EXPLORING IBM TECHNOLOGY, PRODUCTS & SERVICES

Fourth Edition

Other Titles of Interest From Maximum Press

Exploring IBM @server iSeries and Personal Computers, Eleventh Edition: Hoskins, Wilson, 1-885068-39-5

Exploring IBM RS/6000 Computers, Tenth Edition: Hoskins, Davies, 1-885068-42-5

Exploring IBM @server iSeries and AS/400 Computers, Tenth Edition: Hoskins, Dimmick, 1-885068-43-3

Exploring IBM S/390 Computers, Sixth Edition: Hoskins, Coleman, 1-885068-28-X

Building Intranets With Lotus Notes and Domino 5.0: Krantz, 1-885068-41-7

Marketing on the Internet, Fifth Edition: Zimmerman, 1-885068-49-2

Business-to-Business Internet Marketing, Third Edition: Silverstein, 1-885068-50-6

Marketing With E-Mail, Second Edition: Kinnard, 1-885068-51-4

101 Ways to Promote Your Web Site, Second Edition: Sweeney, 1-885068-45-X

Internet Marketing for Less Than $500/Year: Yudkin, 1-885068-52-2

Internet Marketing for Your Tourism Business: Sweeney, 1-885068-47-6

Internet Marketing for Information Technology Companies: Silverstein, 1-885068-46-8

For more information, visit our Web site at *www.maxpress.com* or e-mail us at *moreinfo@maxpress.com*

EXPLORING IBM TECHNOLOGY, PRODUCTS & SERVICES

Fourth Edition

Become an instant insider on IBM's
world of computing solutions

Edited by Jim Hoskins

MAXIMUM PRESS
605 Silverthorn Road
Gulf Breeze, FL 32561
(850) 934-0819
www.maxpress.com
moreinfo@maxpress.com

Publisher: Jim Hoskins
Manager of Finance/Administration: Donna Tryon
Production Manager: ReNae Grant
Cover Design: Lauren Smith Designs
Compositor: PageCrafters Inc.
Copy Editor: Deborah Miller
Proofreader: Kim Stefansson
Indexer: Susan Olason
Printer: P.A. Hutchison

This publication is designed to provide accurate and authoritative information in regard to the subject matter covered. It is sold with the understanding that the publisher is not engaged in rendering professional services. If legal, accounting, medical, psychological, or any other expert assistance is required, the services of a competent professional person should be sought. ADAPTED FROM A DECLARATION OF PRINCIPLES OF A JOINT COMMITTEE OF THE AMERICAN BAR ASSOCIATION AND PUBLISHERS.

Recognizing the importance of preserving what has been written, it is a policy of Maximum Press to have books of enduring value published in the United States printed on acid-free paper, and we exert our best efforts to that end.

Library of Congress Cataloging-in-Publication Data

Hoskins, Jim.
Exploring IBM technology, products & services : become an instant insider on IBM's world of computing solutions / Jim Hoskins, Bill Wilson.— 4th ed.
p. cm.
Includes index.
ISBN 1-885068-62-X (acid-free paper)
1. IBM computers. 2. Computer networks. I. Wilson, Bill, 1951- II. Title.
QA76.8.I1015 E97 2001
004—dc21
00-012964

*To my loving wife Monica
who handles our five kids
and makes it look easy ...*

Acknowledgements

Many people assisted with the creation of this edition including Lisa Dashman, Doug Davies, Roger Dimmick, Cheryl Endres, Ames Nelson, Bill Wilson and Casey Young.

Disclaimer

The purchase of computer software or hardware is an important and costly business decision. While the author and publisher of this book have made reasonable efforts to ensure the accuracy and timeliness of the information contained herein, the author and publisher assume no liability with respect to loss or damage caused or alleged to be caused by reliance on any information contained herein and disclaim any and all warranties, expressed or implied, as to the accuracy or reliability of said information.

This book is not intended to replace the manufacturer's product documentation or personnel in determining the specifications and capabilities of the products mentioned in this book. The manufacturer's product documentation should always be consulted, as the specifications and capabilities of computer hardware and software products are subject to frequent modification. The reader is solely responsible for the choice of computer hardware and software. All configurations and applications of computer hardware and software should be reviewed with the manufacturer's representatives prior to choosing or using any computer hardware and software.

Trademarks

The words contained in this text which are believed to be trademarked, service marked, or otherwise to hold proprietary rights have been designated as such by use of initial capitalization. No attempt has been made to designate as trademarked or service marked any personal computer words or terms in which proprietary rights might exist. Inclusion, exclusion, or definition of a word or term is not intended to affect, or to express judgement upon, the validity of legal status of any proprietary right which may be claimed for a specific word or term.

Table of Contents

Chapter 1:
e-business Basics   1

Chapter 2:
xSeries, Netfinity, NUMA-Q, and PCs   33

Chapter 3:
pSeries and RS/6000 Computers   **85**

Chapter 4:
iSeries and AS/400e Computers   **126**

Chapter 6:
Computer Communications   191

Chapter 7:
IBM Global Services   201

Introduction

> The bravest are surely those who have the clearest vision of what lies before them, glory and danger alike, and yet notwithstanding, go out and meet it.
>
> —*Pericles (c. 495–529 B.C.),*
> *Athenian statesman*

Technology can be daunting. The fast pace of change can leave even technology experts in a daze. However, change means new opportunity. Since luck can be defined as when preparation meets opportunity, those who diligently prepare themselves are likely to find good fortune in the world of technology. This book is your first step in learning about the technology and products of a long-standing industry leader—IBM.

What This Book Is

This book provides an overview of IBM's most popular technologies, products, and services. It provides an overview of IBM's company-wide e-business strategy, the core IBM computer families, computer networking basics, and IBM's services business.

The book includes some excerpts taken from several books published by Maximum Press including:

- Exploring IBM @server xSeries & PCs *(ISBN 1-885068-39-5)*

- Exploring IBM RS/6000 Computers *(ISBN 1-885068-42-5)*

- Exploring IBM @server iSeries & AS/400 Computers *(ISBN 1-885068-43-3)*

- Exploring IBM @server zSeries & S/390 Computers *(ISBN 1-885068-28-X)*

• Exploring IBM Network Stations (*ISBN 1-885068-32-8*)

Consult these separate books for more detailed information on the topics they cover.

What This Book Is Not

This book is not a comprehensive IBM product catalog or a technology encyclopedia. In the fast-moving computer world, any such book would be obsolete before it could be printed. Instead, this book presents basics about e-business, IBM's five computer families, networking, and IBM service offerings. The companion Internet site for this book provides a way to get the most current product information. Finally, this book does not expect you to be an engineer. Business people are typically short on time. Although some technical discussions are necessary, they are as simple and concise as possible while still conveying necessary and useful information.

How to Use This Book

Chapter 1 introduces IBM's e-business strategy. This company-wide thrust is designed to help organizations of all sizes make the most of the Internet and related technology.

Chapter 2 surveys IBM's diverse iSeries and personal computer families including Aptiva, NetVista, Netfinity, and NUMA-Q. It explores the various models, peripherals, and the all-important software that makes these systems work.

Chapter 3 guides you through the pSeries and RS/6000 world. This UNIX-based computer family can be used as a multiuser computer or a high-performance workstation.

Chapter 4 explores IBM's iSeries and the AS/400 computer family. This is IBM's popular mid-range computer family that evolved from the IBM System/3X computer family.

Chapter 5 covers IBM's zSeries and S/390 family. These are the largest computer systems offered by IBM and are used in the most demanding of environments.

Chapter 6 shows how IBM's different computer families can be networked with other computers for the purpose of sharing information, programs, and peripheral equipment.

Chapter 7 introduces IBM's Global Services organization and looks at the types of offerings they provide.

Your "Members Only" Web Site

The world of IBM technology and products changes every day. That is why there is a companion Web site associated with this book. On this site you will find news, expanded information on the topics covered in the book, and other resources of interest.

To get into the companion Web site, go to the Maximum Press Web site located at *www.maxpress.com* and follow the links to the companion Web site for *Exploring IBM Technology, Products, and Services*. You will be asked for a User ID and Password. Type the following:

- For User ID: *ibmtech4e*

- For Password: *tube*

You will then be granted full access to the "Members Only" area. Visit the site often and enjoy the updates and resources with our compliments—and thanks again for buying the book. We ask that you not share the "User ID" and "Password" for this site with anyone else.

1

e-business Basics

The Internet's rise in popularity provides all types of businesses with a new world to pioneer. IBM, which finds itself perfectly positioned in the age of the Internet, is pulling out all the stops to help businesses tame this new frontier. This chapter starts with a quick review of Internet basics and then describes IBM's company-wide vision and strategy for leveraging Internet technology to improve the way the world does business.

What Is the Internet?

The Internet is a public network of computers that spans the globe. What makes the Internet different from private communications networks commonly used by businesses and other institutions is that anyone can get on the Internet. Individuals usually get on the Internet by subscribing to a service offered by an Internet Service Provider (ISP). These are companies that have a computer with a high-speed connection (over leased telephone lines) that allow their subscribers' computers to communicate over the Internet (Figure 1.1). Businesses and institutions often get on the Internet through their own high-

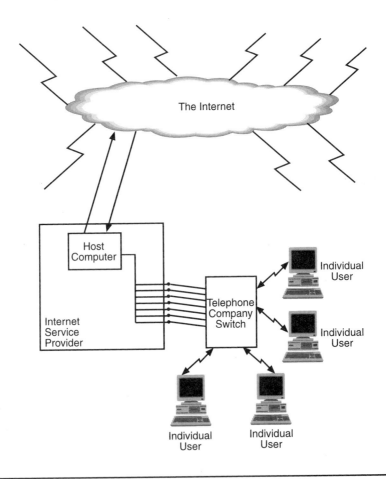

Figure 1.1. Individual Internet users typically access the Internet by dialing into the host computer owned by an Internet Service Provider. The users dial in over standard phone lines and share a high-speed connection between the host computer and the Internet.

speed connection to the Internet that is shared by multiple users within the organization (Figure 1.2).

Where Did the Internet Come From?

The great-grandfather of the Internet was a network called ARPANET developed by the U.S. Department of Defense in 1969 to promote

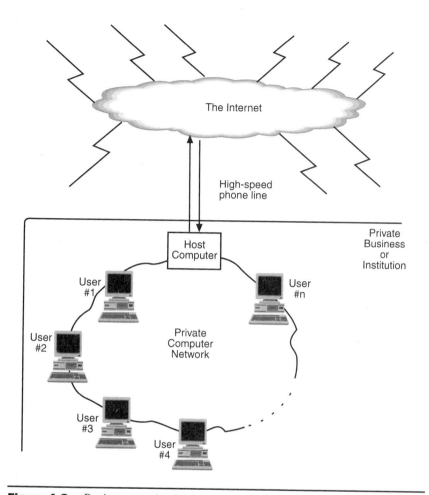

Figure 1.2. Businesses or institutions typically have their own high-speed connection to the Internet, which is shared by multiple users within the organization.

networking research. (See Figure 1.3). Over the years, innovative individuals and government organizations like the National Science Foundation developed and adopted technologies and standards that allowed for the interconnection of all networks that adhered to the standards. The standard communications protocol (i.e., electronic language) used on the Internet since its adoption in 1982 is known as TCP/IP (Transmission Control Protocol/Internet Protocol). By using this common language throughout the Internet, any computer on the

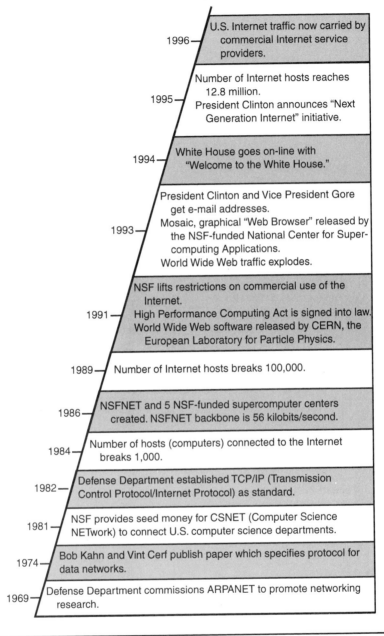

1996 — U.S. Internet traffic now carried by commercial Internet service providers.

1995 — Number of Internet hosts reaches 12.8 million.
President Clinton announces "Next Generation Internet" initiative.

1994 — White House goes on-line with "Welcome to the White House."

1993 — President Clinton and Vice President Gore get e-mail addresses.
Mosaic, graphical "Web Browser" released by the NSF-funded National Center for Super-computing Applications.
World Wide Web traffic explodes.

1991 — NSF lifts restrictions on commercial use of the Internet.
High Performance Computing Act is signed into law.
World Wide Web software released by CERN, the European Laboratory for Particle Physics.

1989 — Number of Internet hosts breaks 100,000.

1986 — NSFNET and 5 NSF-funded supercomputer centers created. NSFNET backbone is 56 kilobits/second.

1984 — Number of hosts (computers) connected to the Internet breaks 1,000.

1982 — Defense Department established TCP/IP (Transmission Control Protocol/Internet Protocol) as standard.

1981 — NSF provides seed money for CSNET (Computer Science NETwork) to connect U.S. computer science departments.

1974 — Bob Kahn and Vint Cerf publish paper which specifies protocol for data networks.

1969 — Defense Department commissions ARPANET to promote networking research.

Figure 1.3. The Internet started as a government project and is now a whole new business frontier.

Internet can communicate with any other computer on the Internet—that is the beauty of standardization. The World Wide Web exists on top of the Internet. While the Internet is a network of computers, the World Wide Web is a collection of "pages" that contain links to other "pages." When you click on a link, you are transmitting your request for another Web page over the Internet. In order to view a Web page, you need to have a browser that understands World Wide Web commands. This browser software, as well as other Internet software (running on all participating computers and using TCP/IP communications) implements the functions available on the Internet such as e-mail.

It's About Content

So, now that we have the Internet, what good is it? Well, it is only as good as the information it delivers. The Internet is like the plumbing going to most people's homes today. No one cares about the pipes themselves—it is the clear, pure, life-giving water the pipes bring that is important. Similarly, it is the text, sound, illustrations, images, and video (collectively called the content) that the Internet brings to your home, school, and business that makes the Internet important—or not. Just as a dirty water system renders your home's plumbing worthless, poor-quality content would make the Internet nothing more than a collection of useless wires. So, if "content is king," where does it come from? Fortunately, the economic and social power represented by the Internet has attracted some of the best minds in the world, who are delivering impressive content.

What sets the Internet apart from other important content delivery infrastructures (e.g., television, radio, and print media) is that the Internet is a two-way communications channel. This allows users to actively make choices that direct the flow of the content to suit their specific needs. It also allows users to communicate with the content provider and with other users—something the traditional media does not offer. This interactive capability allows users to execute transactions (e.g., buying and selling things or making reservations) and share content with others, providing a new way for people to work and play together in cyberspace.

Today's Internet

Today there are, by some estimates, over 330 million people attached to the Internet and that number will grow to close to a billion by the end of 2003, with most of the growth being in non-English speaking countries.

The limitation of speed is one of the biggest challenges facing today's Internet. Due to the communications infrastructure commonly in use today, the Internet often makes users wait for the information they request—sometimes for seconds and too often for minutes. These speed and capacity limitations determine the type and quantity of information that one user (e.g., a business) can send to another (e.g., a customer). As it turns out, the most interesting information like high-resolution graphics, video, and audio represent large bodies of information and therefore move slowly over today's Internet. Today's Internet innovators are keenly aware of this need for more speed and huge efforts are underway to deliver just that. Improved network infrastructure (called Internet2) is under development and will provide a hundred-times to a thousand-times more speed (i.e., bandwidth) than today's Internet. Internet2 is being developed by a group of over 170 U.S. universities. The goal of these universities, along with their government and industry partners, is to enhance the current Internet structure. Internet2 will address speeds on the backbone of the Internet, but much of the slow speed is caused by the slow speed of telephone wires into your home computer.

A new introduction to the Internet environment is the information portal. A portal is a personalized door to the Internet or a company's private network (intranet). It allows a user to determine what information they want displayed to them on their screen and how they want it displayed. This is easier said than done. Much of the information that a person requires to do his or her work is buried in multiple different systems throughout the company. For example, think of an insurance claim process. Policy information is in one data storage area, the claim request is in another, pictures may be stored in a folder in a file cabinet on another floor and audio tapes of interviews somewhere else. Police reports may arrive in paper form, but could probably be accessed via the Internet as well. The portal, through its many layers, retrieves the information that the user requires from disparate sources and displays it as needed.

Pervasive Computing

In addition to the growing number of people accessing the Internet, there are a growing number of information providing devices being attached to the Internet. In fact, there are already more devices than people attached to the Internet. What is emerging is an environment of pervasive computing.

Pervasive computing is all about connecting people and their devices to information they need, whenever and wherever they want to get it. This is the next wave in computing, where every device imaginable—from your cell phone to your car, your washing machine to your wristwatch—is linked to the Internet, intranets, and each other.

There are a number of factors that have come about in the past few years to propel this new paradigm. First, there was the evolution of network computing. Also, as people's lives become more complicated, time becomes a luxury commodity and the desire for convenience grows. This helps to explain the excitement of the Internet, which is being adopted faster and more widely than any other technology in history. In less than a decade, awareness of, access to, and acceptance of the Internet as a daily tool have exploded. These elements have converged to warrant the need and demand for convenient access to all kinds of information.

Pervasive computing is already affecting the way business is conducted in many industries, including telecommunications, banking and finance, travel, and manufacturing. For example, a Japanese telecommunications company has a premium phone model that allows users to touch a menu on the phone screen and reach an array of services, such as stock trading, buying travel and venue tickets, weather, news, phone directories, restaurant guides, and more. A supermarket chain based in the United Kingdom enables customers to do their grocery shopping on a personal digital assistant (PDA), even specifying when they want to pick up the order. A major U.S. supplier to the chemical industry has put meters on their gas holding tanks that communicate directly with the supplier: when the tank reaches a predetermined level of emptiness, the tank "tells" the supplier to send a truck out to refill the tank to capacity.

For individuals, pervasive computing means a level of convenience that promotes increased productivity and flexibility, resulting in a new work style and life style. For businesses, this new paradigm fulfills the promise of e-business, reaching new markets, improving customer satisfaction, reducing cycle times and costs, and providing opportunities for new revenue generation.

What Are People Doing Right Now

There is a flurry of business activity on the Internet going on right now. Here are just a few examples to get you thinking.

- Direct Stock Market is a virtual capital market for small-cap companies that reduces the cost of accessing capital from the primary market. It serves as a meeting ground for investors and entrepreneurs where they can make available online their prospectus, corporate profile, financial statements, and even a virtual road show to a literally limitless audience of small investors.

- Dupont underwent a major information technology re-engineering project improving the way 80,000 employees "communicate, collaborate, and coordinate" for faster decision-making and increased ability to exploit market opportunities.

- Miami Computer Supply is a leading supplier of computer supplies and projection presentation products. They offer their catalog of over 3,000 products to business customers online at www.mcsinet.com to provide their customers with anytime/anywhere purchasing and greatly reduced order transaction costs.

- Mediconsult.com is a virtual medical clinic on the Internet that offers peer-reviewed medical information on more than 50 chronic medical conditions and has logged more than 180,000 patient "visits" a month. It now is expanding beyond consulting and is beginning to sell a line of hard-to-find medical products over the Internet.

- Hoffmaster is a market leader in premium decorative tableware for the institutional marketplace (restaurants, healthcare, education, lodging, etc.). They have placed their catalog online and are now able to reach a much wider universe of customers and have been able to differentiate themselves as a market leader and innovator in a commodity market.

- The American Schools Directory is developing Web sites for all K–12 schools in America. Currently 106,000 participating sites provide information about schools for educators, students, parents, and local communities.

- Wisconsin Gas, a natural gas utility serving more than 500,000 customers, has developed 40 new workflow and collaborative applications to streamline business processes. For example, their Automated Service Application manages all the functions and processes involved in constructing, installing, and servicing gas connections over a corporate intranet.

- Lehigh Valley Safety Shoe Company (a 20-person company) is now doing all of its sales and distribution and wholesale business over the Internet.

- Electric Power Research Institute (EPRI) is a not-for-profit research organization that acts as a research clearinghouse for more than 700 utility companies. It now has a Web site at which members share text, charts, and graphics, making the exchange of ideas more efficient and interactive.

- The State Bar of California now has a Web site where its members can access 15 years' worth of accumulated data from existing databases. The State Bar now posts bar exam results 48 hours earlier than it did previously, provides consumer information for finding a lawyer, and invites public comment on pending state legislation.

- Charles Schwab, a leading discount brokerage company, launched the e.Schwab stock market trading Web site which lets customers access their accounts and place trades from anywhere, 24 hours a day, over the Internet. Schwab did as much business through its Web site in the first year as it did in 13 years with its desktop software offering.

- Chrysler built the Supply Partner Information Network (SPIN), a way for Chrysler to communicate over its corporate intranet with some 20,000 suppliers it relies upon. SPIN also provides a way for suppliers to submit cost-saving ideas, which already has realized $1 billion in cost savings.

- L.L. Bean has gone live with electronic commerce at its Web site. Traffic on the site almost immediately exceeded expectations. During the first holiday shopping season, sales at L.L. Bean's Web site were twice what had been forecast.

- Auto-by-Tel uses the Web to take consumer order descriptions and match them with inventories of more than 1,500 car dealers who subscribe to the service. (They run at a rate of more than 40,000 requests per month, with more than $2 billion in sales generated this way.)

- In Japan, a project called VCALS (Vehicle Computer Assisted Logistic System) is building an electronic commerce environment that will include paperless design processes in a virtual enterprise environment and an electronics parts ordering and digital service manual covering the entire Japanese automotive industry between manufacturers and repair shops.

- In Europe, 30 European automotive and aerospace companies have embarked on a project called AIT (Advanced Information Technology) that intends to make the manufacturing segment more competitive. The initial focus is to define a common infrastructure to support interoperability between user environments.

- Hewitt Associates, a global management consulting leader, delivers HR forms on the Web using IBM's Enterprise Information Portal (EIP) and content management solutions. This has allowed them to improve their client service.

- Within IBM itself, the intranet serves as a connection for nearly 270,000 employees. Users can access more than one million documents about every aspect of IBM business, from customer accounts to engineering specifications. Initially, there were about 62,000 hits per day. Now there are about 6,000,000 hits a day. Using e-business is how IBM works.

It is easy to see how these efforts (and a thousand others like them) are making our lives easier as they permeate education, medicine, manufacturing, entertainment, travel, etc. Over time, the use of Internet technology (and its derivatives) will enable businesses to become more and more competitive through quickly formed online partnerships with those inside or outside the company who can bring value to company projects. The ability to interact, using the Internet standards being established today, will undoubtedly permeate almost every aspect of our lives and businesses.

Through Internet technology, the cost of doing business will decline, much the way costs declined with the proliferation of the telephone and all its adjunct services. The phone brought people together instantly: They no longer had to spend time composing and editing letters, then wait during the time it took the letter to arrive at the addressee and to be answered. As the phone became more and more productive, the cost of doing business decreased. Decisions were reached more quickly. The enormous costs associated with travel diminished as more and more people conducted business on the phone. Business people began to teleconference, further reducing travel costs and time. Customers no longer had to physically walk into a store to make purchases; this could be done on the phone. Today, customers don't have to "walk into" paper catalogs; they can shop on the Internet 24 hours a day, regardless of the weather.

During this transition from "no phones" to "all phones," business executives became more and more aware of the phone's potential, just as they were totally aware of other basic business tools, such as the importance of location and advertising in order to reach customers. Any chief executive officer who, during this transition to an all-telephone world, was not aware of the emergence, the importance, and the impact of the telephone faced the prospect of not only falling behind the competition, but also failing miserably. Similarly today, any CEO who is not aware of the Internet's potential will inevitably be overrun by the giant wave of the technological progress and advantages inherent in the Internet. Seldom do you see a television or print ad without an Internet address. The phrases "e-mail" and "www dot com" are now part of the world's languages, along with expressions like voice mail and fax. Clearly, mainstream business has arrived on the Internet.

IBM's View of e-business

IBM's chairman and CEO, Louis V. Gerstner, Jr., summed up IBM's view of e-business when he said, "The rise of the Internet is connecting people with people, and people with content, in ways that weren't possible just a few years ago. But sheer connectivity, as important as it is, is not, and never has been, the Holy Grail. The payoff is what people and institutions do with this extraordinary capability—which literally has the power to change the way we work, and the way we live."

What IBM and the industry see is not only a business opportunity, but a change in the way businesses and people live today and tomorrow. For all its glamour and hype, the Internet has the potential to make all our lives better.

To capitalize on such potential is a huge undertaking that requires vision, enormous effort, and the talent necessary to thrive in the frontier that is today's Internet. Think of it as electronic covered wagons riding toward new horizons. IBM refers to its broad Internet/intranet initiatives as e-business.

Why Does IBM Like the Internet

IBM views the Internet and its sibling intranets as opportunities for unprecedented growth, not only for businesses around the globe, but for the IBM corporation as well. Both the Internet and intranets are a means for users, large and small, to accomplish some basic business goals: disseminating information, cutting costs, and getting to market faster and more efficiently. At the same time the Internet is a device for accomplishing other things, too: forging tighter relationships with consumers, gaining an advantage over the competition, mobilizing global work forces, integrating supply chains, and reinventing companies. Essentially, IBM perceives the Internet as a chance to help users harness today's newest technologies and achieve surprising goals.

Common sense says users want to do ordinary things over the Internet: check on their bank accounts from home, find the cheapest airline fare without leaving their office or den, get training without walking into a classroom, put in their two cents' worth about local politics—even though it's well past closing time at City Hall.

People also want to perform complex tasks: conduct complicated business transactions with business partners around the globe, stamp out bureaucracy and get teams to work together better and faster, improve efficiency by cutting waste.

Another reason IBM is interested in the Internet is because of results of its own research. IBM has conducted many one-on-one interviews with CEOs; division managers; vice presidents of marketing, sales, customer service; and so on. IBM has also conducted many focus groups with Fortune 1000 business executives, including many non-IT (Information Technology) executives.

Research confirms that the most important business issues relate to growth, revenue, competition, and productivity. The findings also indicate that the Internet is seen as a potentially powerful business tool that can and should be used to help with the issues of growth, revenue, competition, and productivity—a notion expressed even by those with limited Internet experience. Further, the studies found that security concerns are perceived as the final obstacle to Internet commerce: If a user buys something online, the transaction should be secure. If you want to send a private message to someone over the Internet, it should remain private. If you want to see your checking account balance, only you should be able to. Systems should be totally secure and reliable.

Currently, the Internet and the technology it is based on are the driving force behind the most sweeping change in computing history. The push is to move to content (information that includes text, numbers, graphics, images, sound, and video) and programs (used to manipulate content) from a user's personal computer (a client) and onto larger computers (servers) that can be accessed over the Internet. Why? Because there are costs to be saved, productivity to be enhanced, and new markets to enter and expand.

There are as many applications of the Internet and its technology as there are businesses. Below are some of the cost savings that can be realized.

In the past years, personal computers (PCs) have grown more powerful and more complex. This complexity is why studies have estimated that well over half of the cost of using a PC in your business is due to the time spent managing the PC—installing, upgrading, troubleshooting, helping users, and so on.

The cost of managing a large pool of high-powered PCs can be reduced by storing more, but not all, of the content and programs users need on a server shared by all the users. This centralized content and software can then be secured, diagnosed, repaired, updated, and otherwise managed once (on the server), rather than many times (once for each client).

The Internet's World Wide Web function is built around this centralized approach. The user needs only one program (a Web browser) to access any of the content offered on the World Wide Web. In fact, any type of computer—an IBM PC, Apple Macintosh, UNIX workstation, etc.—equipped with a Web browser program can access any of the content—and can even run programs (written in languages like Java) offered on the Internet. Since the same functions are available no matter what type of computer system or operating system you are using, the Web represents a threat to the dominance of Microsoft Windows and Intel microprocessors.

Until standards were imposed by the widespread adoption of the Internet, programmers and the businesses that paid them were in a never-ending struggle to make one type of computer system on one type of network that could share information with another type of computer on yet another type of network. Today the Internet has a set of rules, and since everyone uses the same set of protocols, content is viewable by all.

So, there are many benefits to standardizing and centralizing content as well as some of the programs. To centralize content, you must have a large-scale, powerful, secure, and reliable computer systems (and the services to back them up) to act as servers (the points of centralization), and the tools to manage the sophisticated networks through which users access content.

Why is this important to IBM? As a long-time leader in the large-computer arena, IBM is well positioned to help businesses implement their plans for leveraging the Internet to improve business results—a fact IBM is keenly aware of. As a result, every major segment of IBM is aggressively aligning its strategies, products, services, and development priorities with the company's new Internet strategy. IBM's professional services organization—the fastest-growing part of IBM—is better equipped than ever to provide the expertise and personnel to help design, implement, and manage these large-scale computing solutions.

In fact, IBM's Global Services unit is the world's largest consulting business. And, since approximately 70 percent of the world's data resides on IBM computer systems, who is in a better position than IBM to help users enable their business information and processes for the Internet world?

While IBM is often a strong competitor in the low-end commodity world—PCs, terminals, printers, etc.—IBM is at its best when there are large-scale problems to be solved (e.g., such as designing powerful server hardware or secure and reliable software, handling a large volume of transactions, etc.). These are the reasons that IBM is excited about the current trend toward centralization being driven by the Internet and intranets.

Creating a leadership position in the development of Internet—based computing solutions is a top priority for IBM CEO Lou Gerstner. IBM's Internet Division, under the leadership of Dr. Irving Wladawsky—Berger since 1995, has been working across all of IBM's individual units helping to define and implement IBM's software-based Internet and e-business initiatives. The Internet Division is also responsible for branding, product integration, and marketing.

Another major move that bolstered IBM's ability to go after the opportunities presented by the rise of the Internet was the purchase of Lotus Development Corporation in July 1995. The unique combination of Lotus's end-user software expertise and IBM's scalable enterprise systems experience enable us to quickly address brand, product, and technology-integration issues, thus leveraging the strengths of both companies and giving IBM a significant lead in the groupware world. With the advent of Domino, Lotus brings the substantial capabilities of Notes to the World Wide Web and further strengthens IBM's Internet hand. The strategy is working, because sales of Lotus Notes/Domino are up.

A second major company purchase has increased IBM's offerings in systems management and security. Tivoli is a company that specializes in the management of diverse applications and systems. They have developed an Application Management Specification (AMS) that is in line with the industry-standard MIF format described by the Desktop Management Task Force (DMTF). AMS allows companies to manage the deployment and monitoring of diverse applications, even those purchased off the shelf such as Microsoft Office. SecureWay has been moved under the Tivoli umbrella to couple application security with application development.

Where Do Intranets Fit In?

Businesses are establishing intranets at a phenomenal rate, which indicates a burgeoning opportunity. As companies build intranets for improving internal communications, streamlining processes such as purchasing, and simplifying transaction processing, they are finding multiple sources of business value. They are reducing communication costs, increasing productivity and sales, and significantly improving the quality of work.

Today, businesses are only scratching the surface of the wealth of possibilities offered by intranets. Intranets allow companies to reengineer processes as well as expand their business because of improved communications and greater productivity. Knight Ridder SourceOne, for example, quickly delivers documents—some rare and obscure—from internal digital and hard copy libraries from prestigious affiliated institutions around the world. Leveraging intranet technology, Knight Ridder SourceOne yielded impressive gains in efficiency and customer satisfaction. Further, companies such as Mason and Hanger, an engineering contracting company, are prototyping intranets for decision support systems. These are just two examples of the many intranet projects under way at businesses and institutions around the globe.

Many businesses that already have intranets up and running are quickly finding a need to securely provide outside trading partners with access to their intranet via the Internet. Intranets that allow select groups access over the Internet are called extranets. Businesses seem to be evolving intranets into extranets quickly.

Companies may be tempted to jump on the intranet bandwagon using the fastest means possible. This tactic may meet some basic requirements, but it often does not take into account future network growth, the advantages gained by leveraging existing data, or how to add new intranet-enhancing products as they become available. These considerations demand that intranets be flexible, open, and integrated. In addition, any time a company makes information accessible to a wide group of people or extends an intranet to suppliers or vendors, it must establish appropriate security mechanisms, rangi... firewalls (a computer system used to electronically isolate a con... intranet from the Internet) to control access to encryption (dig... encoding information to prevent unauthorized viewing). So ho... IBM positioned to go after this intranet opportunity?

IBM has been managing and connecting enterprise computing environments for more than two decades. Many of IBM's worldwide loyal customers now want to reap the rewards that intranet technology can bring. IBM is helping these long-standing customers implement intranets and using these successes to go after new customers.

IBM has the experience along with the depth and breadth of skills to help companies get intranets up and running quickly. IBM is focusing on creating new and tangible value for businesses on the Internet using a security-rich, integrated approach. The company is leveraging its line of security products and technologies to help users build intranets that will safely handle mission-critical data and tasks. IBM's time-tested security products and technologies, combined with offerings from both IBM and its wholly owned subsidiary Lotus, will allow IBM to effectively compete in everything from the smallest departmental intranet to complex intranets connecting worldwide enterprises.

IBM research indicates that one of every three companies are pursuing a strategy of revolutionary, as opposed to evolutionary, change. The business environment has become so competitive and customer expectations so high that it is a rare company that excels by doing business as usual. The competitive nature of business has led today's users to expect the highest quality at the lowest cost with impeccable service. Traditionally, most companies emphasized only one of three areas: quality, cost, or service. To thrive today, it is imperative that they be strong in all three.

An IBM study of hundreds of senior functional and information technology executives found that when companies don't take advantage of breakthrough advances, they limit their ability to keep pace with their competitors that do leverage technology. This yields a business cultural imperative: "change or die." Subjects in the study indicate that to get the most out of the change, it needs to be fast—at least as fast as competitors—and much deeper than cosmetic adjustments.

IBM understands the nature of this transformation not only as a supplier to businesses around the globe, but also through its own experience in the marketplace and its internal alterations in recent years.

and intranets serve as the impetus for positive change
.e. They have laid the groundwork for a surge of busi-
.ormations transcending industry, geography, and size.
.npanies are fundamentally interested in intranets for enabling,
.ncing, and extending effective communications with and among
.ganizational communities of interest. There can be mutual benefits
derived from intranet working between synergistic businesses.
Intranets also have allowed companies to enter new areas in their
industry and expand elements within their businesses. Internet technology employed in intranets can be the base that a business uses to
reinvent its entire operation.

This volatile but fertile business environment is the backdrop for
IBM's e-business strategy. Every IBM offering in this arena is designed
to optimize, expand, or transform new channels of business value.
This translates into businesses' successfully reengineering, broaden-
ing their scope, adding new areas of competence, and enhancing the
way people communicate with one another.

Next, we examine the specific direction IBM is taking in addressing opportunities offered by the current mass migration to the Internet and intranets.

IBM's e-business Cycle

Simply stated, IBM's e-business strategy is designed to create new
value for businesses through the Internet and Internet technology. In
IBM's view, a traditional business can become a successful and thriv-
ing e-business by going through the e-business cycle. This cycle consists of four stages as depicted in Figure 1.4.

- Transform: In this stage, a business is focused on finding new
  and innovative ways to leverage Internet technology to improve
  core business processes. The challenge is to exploit the new
  and dramatic options for doing things like managing customer
  and employee relations, unifying the supply chain, and conducting online business transactions. This phase requires
  e-business vision, planning, design, and integration skills all
  managed to help achieve maximum business value.

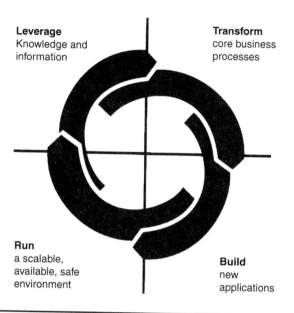

Figure 1.4. The e-business cycle.

- Build: During this period, a business is busy creating and deploying new e-business applications identified in the "Transform" stage. Activities include things like developing Web sites, integrating systems and data, serving Web-based users, and providing for security and privacy. IBM's Application Framework for e-business (covered later in this chapter) provides a structure on which these new e-business applications can be built adhering to widely adopted standards to provide flexibility.

- Run: In this stage, e-business applications have become mission critical and must therefore be executed in a stable, reliable, and secure systems environment available 24 hours a day, 7 days-a-week. Here is where the focus is on choosing and operating the correct computer hardware, software, and network necessary to thrive in the e-business world. Each of IBM's server families is described in subsequent chapters.

- Leverage: Now that e-business applications are deployed and running in a reliable, available, and secure environment, it is time to leverage the knowledge and information flowing in from customers, suppliers, and business partners. Sophisticated business intelligence and knowledge management discipline are used to glean business value from large bodies of information gathered online over time. The intent is to anticipate customer needs, assess profitability, identify new business opportunities, assess risk, detect fraud, etc.

The Foundation Supporting IBM's e-business Strategy

We have seen how IBM is defining today's users needs through the three application groupings: commerce, intranet/extranet, and content management. Now we can take a quick look at some underlying infrastructure components upon which IBM delivers its Internet/intranet offerings:

- Application framework for e-business

- WebSphere Software Platform (an implementation of the application framework for e-business)

- Java, the key to independence

- XML, metadata for e-business

- IBM server hardware

- Security and application management

Application Framework for e-business

IBM's Application Framework for e-business is a software roadmap for those who will be developing Internet- or intranet-based application programs (i.e., independent software developers, IBM business partners, IBM customers, etc.). It is an architecture based on industry standards that provides a foundation upon which software developers can efficiently develop e-business applications that link people, information, and business processes to a Web site.

The key e-business applications within the framework fall into one of three categories:

Application Server Software

Products in this category provide the environment in which e-business applications function. These include products that enable a business to integrate applications (existing and new) and business processes with partners, suppliers, and customers. Examples of products in this category include the IBM MQSeries, Lotus Domino, IBM WebSphere, and DB2 Universal Database.

Development Tools and Components

Software in this category includes tools that help application programmers build and modify e-business applications. Also included in this category are connector products that allow new e-business applications to be linked to existing (i.e., legacy) applications which house key business data. Examples of products in this category include IBM VisualAge, Domino Designer, IBM WebSphere Studio, SanFrancisco, e-Suite, and Enterprise Information Portal (EIP).

Secure Network and Management Software

Doing real business over the Internet is only desirable if security is insured. Products in this category of the framework address this need for security. Further, the e-business environment presents some unique systems management challenges that are addressed by these products. Example of products in this category include Tivoli systems management software and Tivoli SecureWay family of security tools.

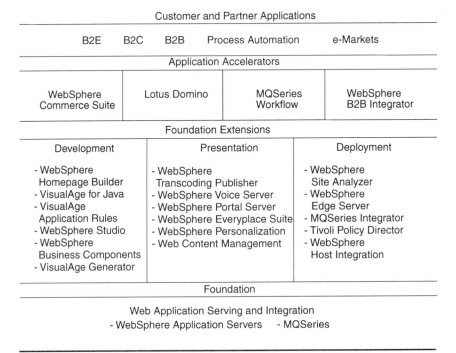

Customer and Partner Applications				
B2E	B2C	B2B	Process Automation	e-Markets

Application Accelerators			
WebSphere Commerce Suite	Lotus Domino	MQSeries Workflow	WebSphere B2B Integrator

Foundation Extensions		
Development	Presentation	Deployment
- WebSphere Homepage Builder - VisualAge for Java - VisualAge Application Rules - WebSphere Studio - WebSphere Business Components - VisualAge Generator	- WebSphere Transcoding Publisher - WebSphere Voice Server - WebSphere Portal Server - WebSphere Everyplace Suite - WebSphere Personalization - Web Content Management	- WebSphere Site Analyzer - WebSphere Edge Server - MQSeries Integrator - Tivoli Policy Director - WebSphere Host Integration

Foundation
Web Application Serving and Integration - WebSphere Application Servers   - MQSeries

Figure 1.5. The WebSphere Software Platform strategy divides the IBM software products into four main groups.

WebSphere Software Platform

In June of 2000, IBM announced the WebSphere Software Platform as an implementation of their e-business application framework. IBM continues to update its software platform by increasing consolidation of many specific products into solution suites. The WebSphere Software Platform allows IBM customers to purchase the tools they need with a greater understanding of where they fit in the overall IBM e-business strategy.

Built on the WebSphere brand, the platform strategy divides the IBM software products into four main groups: Foundation, Foundation Extensions, Application Accelerators, and Customer and Partner Applications. (Figure 1.5) The Foundation group is composed of products that provide content for Internet applications, such as WebSphere Application Servers. These servers contain hooks to content repositories such as DB2 UDB.

The Foundation Extensions are further divided into Development, Presentation, and Deployment buckets. The development tools comprise products needed to make content accessible to the Internet, such as VisualAge for Java. The presentation group includes products that make content available to the Internet, such as Enterprise Information Portal. This group includes both browser presentation of Internet content, as well as presentation of content through pervasive devices. The final group, deployment, includes tools that make the business application available to these different devices, managing deployment to servers and assessment of existing applications. This group includes products such as Tivoli Policy Director.

Application Accelerators are integrated products that can be used to build a specific type of application rapidly. For example, with WebSphere Commerce Suite, a customer can quickly develop a store-front application on the Web. This suite comes with components to manage the catalog, payment, security, etc. required for an Internet store-front application.

The final level, Customer and Partner Applications, are those applications built by IBM partners that are ready for the customer to implement. These applications are built on IBM software and provide the mechanism for such things as business-to-business (B2B) applications.

XML, the Key to e-business Metadata

Hyper Text Markup Language (HTML) is based on the Standardized General Markup Language (SGML) and emerged along with the World Wide Web. It is a language associated with Web page content that tells the browser how that item is to be displayed on the screen. Released in 1986, it now is in its fourth version. In the following example,
    $5.98
indicates that the price "$5.98" should be displayed on the screen in bold. However, it does not explain what the amount $5.98 means.

Metadata is a term that means data about data. It first came in vogue in the early 1990s with the development of large data warehouses for business intelligence and data mining. Business intelligence users needed to understand where the data came from that they were looking at, as well as what underlying formulas contributed to the information. It was the only way they could make sound business decisions.

Companies have been sending information to each other for many years using a format called Electronic Data Interchange (EDI). This format insured that the receiving company could tell where the information they needed was in the file by its record type, location on the record, and physical description (type, length, etc.).

While sufficient for the time, EDI was not sufficient for the booming Web commerce. There were too many meetings and too much time required for companies to agree on record formats and definitions. Applications needed to be developed in Web time, not data warehouse time. HTML was no help because it only described how to show the object, not what it meant or what its physical characteristics were. Enter XML.

Extended Markup Language (XML) is also derived from SGML. It is similar to HTML, but its function is to define an element, not tell how it should be displayed. For example.

<price of tie>$5.98<price of tie>

tells us that $5.98 is the price of a tie, not the monthly office supplies cost. There are agreed upon standards for much of the general XML language, but discussions still go on. In addition, there have been multiple industry sub-XML groups that have come to agreements about terms commonly used in their industries, such as policy number and claim number for the insurance industry. These extensions of XML, are called XML applications or document type definitions (DTDs). These standards have their own names, such as the Chemical Markup Language (CML),

The downside of XML? Size. Every item that is sent from one company to another needs a description. This description takes up a lot of space, making large transmission files larger than they already are. Nonetheless, with the rapidity of its adoption, it fills the need that apparently has been around for a while.

Java, the Key to Independence

Java technology is a central part of IBM's overall e-business strategy because it gives users more flexibility, offers economies to software developers, and tends to loosen the iron grip of proprietary operating systems (such as Microsoft Windows) and computer system implementations (Intel microprocessors) in favor of open industry standards. Java promises to let any computer exchange information with any other computer, a long-sought-after goal in business computing. Here is how it accomplishes this.

Java technology was announced by Sun Microsystems in 1995 and is now strongly supported by additional companies including IBM, Netscape, and Novell. Java technology consists of two basic elements: the Java programming language used by a programmer to write programs for users, and the Java-enabled browser software that runs Java programs on the user's computer (i.e., the Java Virtual Machine).

There are many programming languages available today, but what sets Java apart from the others is that a program written in Java (a derivative of the C++ language) can be run on any type of computer system. With traditional programming languages, the programmer writes a program that is then compiled (translated) into digital codes that can be executed only by a particular computer—the one targeted by the particular compiler used. With Java, the programmer writes the program in much the same way, but it is then translated into Java byte codes, which can be executed on any type of computer running a Java-enabled browser program. It is this Java-enabled browser program on the user's computer that does the final translation from Java byte codes to the digital codes that are actually executed on the particular computer in use. This is how any Java program can run on any type of computer system—because the Java-enabled browser on each user's computer system does the final step in the translation.

You will recall that browser programs (most of which are now Java-enabled) are needed to access an Internet (or intranet) Web site. A programmer can write a Java application (called an applet) and put it up on a Web site. Anyone using a Java-enabled browser (running on any type of computer) who visits that Web site can automatically download and run that Java application program by clicking on a hypertext link. This gets us close to software perfection—the programmer writes an application program (in Java) one time and distributes it over the Internet, where it can be downloaded (with virtually no distribution costs) and run on any type of computer system (one version for all). Since the Java language was designed for delivery over networks, the resulting programs are compact to allow quick downloads to the user's computer.

For users, Java promises-as-you-go simplicity with no upgrade headaches to manage. Users may even purchase a low-cost, simplified computer called a network computer that is capable of running only Java applications resident on a Web server (either on the Internet or an intranet).

IBM is betting heavily on Java technology. In December 1995, IBM first announced its licensing of Java technology. IBM then formed the Center for Java Technology in Hursley, England, to deploy Java technology throughout the IBM product line, including key operating systems (e.g., AIX, OS/2, OS/390, and OS/400), databases (e.g., DB2 UDB), groupware (e.g., Lotus Notes), transaction systems (e.g., CICS), and development tools (e.g., VisualAge). IBM also created Java Validation Centers, where Java program developers can test their programs on Java systems from companies like Sun, HP, IBM, and others at no charge.

IBM has also licensed some related technologies from Sun including JavaOS and HotJava. JavaOS is a compact operating system that can be used in things like cell phones and network computers (simplified, low-cost computers that get their programming from an intranet or the Internet). HotJava was one of the first browser applications, but from the market perspective, has generally been eclipsed by Netscape and Microsoft Explorer. A Java Bean is a reusable software component that can be changed by using drag and drop technology of selected development tools. The Java family is constantly growing. In addition to Java applets, there are Java servlets for use on application servers, Java Database Connectivity (JDBC) for access to different databases, including DB2 UDB and Oracle, and JavaServer Pages (JSP) to aid in creation of Web pages.

Server Hardware

It is the job of the server to offer resources (e.g., Web content, disk space, transaction processing, access to other networks, etc.) to clients (e.g., an individual using a PC to access resources available on the network). Although the terms server and client are applicable to any type of computer network, for our purposes we will concentrate on the Internet/intranet environment.

IBM has four main families of computer systems appropriate for use as Internet or intranet servers. The later chapters in this book explore each of these computer families more closely:

- IBM @server xSeries (including Netfinity and NUMA-Q)

- IBM @server pSeries (including RS/6000)

- IBM @server iSeries (including AS/400)

- IBM @server zSeries (including System/390)

Security

Few Internet subjects are more important than security. To make e-business successful, users must be certain that transactions and communications can be conducted securely. One of the major cornerstones of transacting business on the Internet is the notion that one's business can be truly private and restricted to specific eyes, very much like the mail we send and receive or the phone conversations we have. As a result, security on the Internet is a major consideration for today's businesses, regardless of their size or scope.

The subject of security involves more than a safe connection to worldwide networks. Surveys have indicated that most businesses incur losses that could be prevented because computer viruses infect their business systems, or individuals have inappropriate access to sensitive information. Such losses have cost businesses millions of dollars in lost revenue and productivity. Essentially, business cannot be effectively conducted on the Internet without security.

Here again, IBM's heritage gives it advantages in the all-important area of Internet/intranet security. For years, the company has helped companies control access to mainframes, and today IBM continues to help them secure information across distributed networks around the globe. Thus, in the arena of security, the company has a reputation for innovation and leadership. It has skilled security consultants, technology that has been awarded numerous patents, experience in security services, and the tools necessary for conducting business.

In December 1996 at Internet World in New York City, IBM introduced a broad security framework for conducting business online—called SecureWay. This framework makes it possible for diverse security offerings to work together, allowing businesses to mix and match security products. SecureWay, now part of the Tivoli family of products, provides the easy adoption of new and existing technologies; at the same time, it does not disturb existing cryptographic and other security functions and operations. It does this by effectively isolating an application from the unique properties of a specific recovery implementation.

A Story of Three Businesses

So far, we have covered many pieces of the e-business puzzle. To see how all these pieces can come together to solve problems and create new business opportunities, let's look at hypothetical companies—small, medium, and large—as they investigate and implement Internet technology. By doing so, you can get some ideas on how Internet technology might be used at three different businesses. (Please note that these names and business are fictitious. Any similarity to persons and companies is purely coincidental.)

Small Business—Ned Connolly's Auto Parts

Ned Connolly's Auto Parts is a small distributor of high-performance automobile engine parts for American cars. For the past eight years, Connolly's has been comfortably profitable and growing steadily under Ned Connolly's leadership. Connolly's started by selling a basic line of high-performance auto parts through direct mail in Phoenix, Arizona. Now, they offer an expanded line of parts through direct mail and advertising in regional newspapers and magazines. Over the years, Connolly's has earned a reputation for low prices and speedy delivery. Their customers include the major auto parts chain stores and many independents. They have ten employees who work from a large warehouse. Connolly's currently uses a few personal computers for basic accounting and mailing list management.

Like any good businessperson, Ned is always looking for ways to reach new markets. Ned's daughter introduces him to the Internet one weekend, and Ned begins to think of ways to use this new technology in his business. He has been looking for a way to sell his parts to more people throughout the United States and Canada. In fact, he also would like to start selling his line to European and Japanese dealers who need American auto parts—a strong and fast-growing market. Ned begins to think that the Internet might help him reach these new markets, but he is not knowledgeable about computer technology.

Ned decides to contact a computer consultant in his area who is recommended by a friend. The consultant comes in and spends some time learning about the way Connolly's Auto Parts currently does business and their plans for the future. After careful consideration, the consultant recommends that Connolly's Auto Parts develop a Web site and then launch a marketing campaign to inform new customers about their current strengths (low prices and fast delivery) and secure and convenient online shopping. After reviewing several alternatives, Ned selects the WebSphere Application Server as the foundation for his new Web site. Ned retains the consultant to develop the Web site, including a service for customers looking for answers to commonly asked auto parts questions.

After the site is up and functioning, Ned hires an Internet publicist to announce and promote his new online store. The first thing the publicist does is get Connolly's Online listed in the many online directories and search engines (e.g., Yahoo!, Lycos, Excite, etc.). After this is done, the online publicist begins posting information about the new store in the automotive-oriented areas of the Internet and online services (i.e., news groups, mailing lists, forums, etc.). The online publicist also negotiates links to Connolly's online store from heavily traveled Web sites that cater to auto enthusiasts.

As online visitors (from all over the world) begin to arrive at Connolly's Online, they are greeted by grand opening specials featuring prices and terms sure to keep buyers coming back. Ned and his staff can easily manage the online store (change prices, add products, etc.) from a personal computer at their convenience. Ned selected the WebSphere Application Server because he was able to develop the program in under 60 days and he knew he could depend on the reliability of the IBM solution to maintain his Web site online, 365 days a year, 24 hours a day.

Medium Business—Blue Sky Musical Instruments

Blue Sky is a medium-sized manufacturer of high-quality musical instruments sold throughout the world. The business employs 270 people and has shown consistent growth during its 12-year history. When Blue Sky was a smaller company with only one location, internal communication among employees and from management to employees had been done through traditional means including phone calls, face-to-face meetings, and a company newsletter. However, now that Blue Sky has grown considerably and has spread out into three different locations, internal communications have become more complicated, and sometimes problematic. So Bill Thompson, Blue Sky's president, commissions a task force to investigate the internal communication situation and make recommendations. After conducting extensive employee interviews, the task force finds that company news and word of personnel policy changes is often slow to circulate among employees. This lack of communication sometimes causes personnel problems and generally erodes morale.

The task force also finds that teams consisting of engineers, programmers, and quality personnel, who have been assembled to develop a new line of electronic keyboards, are frustrated. It seems that the team members, often selected from more than one company site due to their unique skills, have difficulty coordinating their activities. Telephone tag, time zone differences, frequent trips between company sites, and mail problems all result in delays in their development schedules.

The task force concludes that Blue Sky had grown to a point where their existing internal communications methods no longer meet the needs of the business. The recommendation is to implement an intranet, which can be used as a whole new internal communications infrastructure. The Domino server is recommended for the intranet Web site because of its broadcast and collaboration capabilities. Domino, along with the new intranet Web site, allows Blue Sky to communicate instantly detailed information about company happenings or policy changes directly to employees. The development team members use the discussion database, e-mail, and shared document capabilities of Domino to work together online and reduce frustrating delays.

With the approval and active support of president Bill Thompson, a team is assembled and the intranet project is carefully planned and implemented with the help of an authorized Lotus business partner firm. Although the implementation runs into several hitches along the way, the final result helps improve communications in the ways anticipated. There are also some unanticipated benefits that resulted from this intranet project. For example, a college co-op employee uses Domino's workflow functions to implement an electronic expense-report routing system that streamlines the processing of employee travel-expense reports.

Now that personnel from various functions within Blue Sky better understand what the intranet can do, new ideas for improvement are surfacing regularly. Blue Sky now wonders how they ever did without their company intranet.

Large Business—Markham Associates

Markham, a large insurance consulting company, sells off-site insurance management services for large companies. Markham's strategy is to supply the lowest cost for their customers, reduce fraudulent insurance claims and provide excellent service to their claimants. It has been in business for nearly 20 years and has an excellent reputation. Because their clientele have thousands of employees, Markham has many applications on a S/390 parallel sysplex configuration, including an IMS policy database, a DB2 UDB claims database, and an Oracle data warehouse. Video and audio data are housed in a Content Management database.

As an evolving e-business, Markham has already implemented an online inquiry system for claimants. This has saved the company money on every inquiry and adds up to enormous savings every year.

Markham has recently experienced significant competition and needs to further lower costs. A study shows they are losing many hours coordinating information from their different data stores. Every time they have to go to a new application, they have to get off of their current system and log into a new one. They would like to be able to view all data about a particular claim at the same time. They have heard about Internet portals and think this may be a solution to their problem.

Since Markham currently has a large investment in S/390 hardware, IMS and DB2 software, they check with IBM regarding their portal solutions. IBM informs them that they have the Enterprise Information Portal (EIP) that will help solve their problem. With this product and the appropriate connectors Markham can provide access to its disparate data sources. Using Plumtree's portal presentation interface, Markham's users can take advantage of EIP's federated search and categorization services. When claim information is required, Markham's users can issue a single query from a single logon and retrieve the information they need from all the data stores.

Markham expects to significantly reduce their costs using EIP since the time to gather information will be reduced. They also expect to improve fraud detection by taking advantage of EIP's categorization services.

2

---

xSeries, Netfinity, NUMA-Q, and PCs

This chapter looks at the very popular line of systems which have evolved from the Intel-based personal computer world. This broad family ranges from desktop models for the home to high-performance servers.

A Glance Backwards

IBM entered the small-computer business on August 12, 1981, when an informal part of IBM (called an independent business unit) in Boca Raton, Florida, announced the IBM Personal Computer (IBM PC). The IBM PC was an experiment conducted by 12 developers under the leadership of Philip (Don) Estridge. The small computer system was designed in 12 months from off-the-shelf components. Designed primarily for small to medium-size businesses, the IBM PC had an 8088 microprocessor, 16K of standard memory, 160K diskette drives, a text-only monochrome display, and a cassette port. How undemanding we were in 1981!

Today, a personal computer with such characteristics would not satisfy a preschooler playing games, let alone any serious business needs. However, at that time it fit the needs of users. Not even the 12 developers working on the original IBM PC project imagined that the seed they planted with the IBM PC would grow to become a cornerstone in businesses of all types.

As time went on, IBM developed a family of personal computers, and the independent business unit became a full division, the Entry Systems Division (ESD). IBM published all of the PCs technical information, inviting third-party manufacturers to develop and market their own hardware and software for the PC which they did. This practice of publishing technical details about a product is known as adopting an open architecture policy. As more and more third-party hardware and software became available for the PC family of computers, their popularity grew, prompting even more third-party development activity. This self-fueling cycle was beneficial to IBM, third-party developers, and end users. The success of the open architecture policy has prompted IBM to continue publishing technical details about all subsequent personal computer systems.

The personal computer family included a wide range of products in terms of both function and price. Below we examine the two core PC family members: the Personal Computer XT, shown in Figure 2.1, and the Personal Computer AT, shown in Figure 2.2.

Figure 2.1. IBM Personal Computer XT.

Figure 2.2. IBM Personal Computer AT.

The Personal Computer XT was based on the 8088 microprocessor used in the original PC. It was the first PC family member to support a fixed disk. The Personal Computer AT introduced the 80286 microprocessor to the PC family. It offered enhancements in the areas of performance, disk storage, and memory size.

Many of the other PC family members, such as the IBM 3270 PC, the IBM PC/370, and the IBM Portable PC, were developed directly from these core PC family members. All of these PC family members retained a high degree of software compatibility with preceding products.

On April 2, 1987, IBM announced a new generation of personal computers called Personal System/2 (PS/2) computers. The first four models of the IBM PS/2 family (models 30, 50, 60, and 80) were announced on that day. Over the next few years, the PS/2 family grew to include many different models and configurations. The current PS/2 family is part of IBM's enhanced desktop line and employs the best of IBM's technology and design. It is intended for use by small, medium, and large businesses. Not long after the PS/2 announcement, the Personal System/1 (PS/1) family of computers was introduced and targeted at individuals and small-business users, being sold primarily through retail outlets.

Then, in September 1992, IBM turned its Entry Systems Division into the IBM PC Company. This reorganization was designed to give the personal computer portion of IBM more autonomy and flexibility. On the heels of this reorganization (in October 1992) came the introduction of the ValuePoint and ThinkPad families of personal computers. The ValuePoint family also intended for small, medium, and large business users has been IBM's low-cost, industry-standard line of personal computers. The ThinkPad family consists of battery-powered notebook and subnotebook computers for those needing to compute outside the office.

The biggest change in the use of PCs in the last few years has been the rapid movement to get connected to the public network of networks called the Internet (and private networks based on the same technology, called intranets). Whether we connect by modem from home or through a LAN (local area network) at work, the Internet is changing the way we communicate, share information, and do business. This chapter introduces you to IBM's PC solutions, from connecting to the Web (the World Wide Web, or WWW) at home to building an Internet PC server for businesses. As you will learn, IBM's PC systems have taken on a unique functional and brand identity with IBM's current organization known as the IBM Personal Systems Group.

In May of 2000 IBM introduced its new NetVista family of desktop computers featuring their new sleek designs and Internet readiness. We expect IBM to expand, as time goes on, and incorporate most of the IBM PC family and its network computer family of computers under this new brand name.

Meanwhile, in 1992, a company called Sequent Computers launched a massive design project based on the Intel/personal computing platform but intended to overcome common limitations in computer hardware architectures of the day. The ambitious goals of the project were to:

- Allow system designers to choose freely between networked-servers, symmetric multiprocessing, and clustered architectures as needed.

The result of the project was the NUMA (Non-Uniform Memory Access) architecture that is becoming more popular today and is used all over the world. NUMA uses advanced hardware and software that allows large numbers of processors to operate as a single system while maintaining the ease of programming and manageability of a small system. The NUMA-Q systems use up to 64 Intel microprocessors (with plans to use 256 processors in the future) for a wide variety of e-business related applications, including data warehousing and Web serving. For this reason, they are designed to handle unpredictable workloads (e.g., spikes in online traffic). Many of the world's largest Oracle databases and application environments run on Sequent/IBM NUMA-Q servers.

In October of 1998, Sequent Computer Systems became a founding member of Project Monterey, an IBM-led initiative to create a high-volume, enterprise-ready, commercial UNIX operating system supporting both the PowerPC (used on RS/6000 systems) and Intel architectures. SCO and Intel also were original members. Project Monterey has since expanded to include many leading software vendors and systems manufacturers. Project Monterey is a major UNIX operating system initiative. As part of this initiative, a UNIX operating system is being developed for Intel's IA-64 using IBM's AIX operating system's enterprise capabilities complemented with technology from SCO's UnixWare and the NUMA-Q DYNIX/ptx operating systems. The goal is to create a single UNIX operating system product line that runs on Intel (IA-32, IA-64) and POWER (used in RS/6000 systems) microprocessors, in computers that range from entry-level to large enterprise servers. This 64-bit Monterey/64 UNIX will continue to use the AIX name and has been available since before the launch of Intel's first IA-64 microprocessor, Itanium, in 2001. AIX 5L is currently available for both the RS/6000 and IBM pSeries (PowerPC architecture) and IA-64 based systems, including future NUMA-Q models.

On July 12, 1999, IBM and Sequent announced that they had entered into a merger agreement. The merger brought together unique hardware and software technologies with global presence and partnerships, advancing IBM's thrust in UNIX and NT servers. As a result of the merger, IBM's worldwide sales force sells Sequent's NUMA-Q 1000 and 2000 line under the new IBM NUMA-Q brand.

This new server brand complements IBM's scalable RS/6000 line of servers. In addition, IBM plans to integrate Sequent technologies into IBM products for e-businesses, emerging "NetGen" companies, and UNIX and NT customers.

Many enterprises use both UNIX and NT servers, and this trend is expected to increase over time. The NUMA-Q technology helps UNIX and NT interoperate on a single system. Users can choose to run UNIX applications on some processors within a system while running NT applications on other processors at the same time. The system can be managed from a single point, and data can be shared between the UNIX and NT applications.

Then in October of 2000, IBM introduced the new IBM @server family of computers. This new branding of IBM servers is intended to emphasize IBM's commitment to e-business as well as simplify the entire server line of products. As a result, the new IBM @server xSeries became the new brand name under which all future versions of Netfinity and NUMA-Q servers will be released. The rest of this chapter looks at today's family of Netfinity, PC, and NUMA-Q servers.

Meet the PC Families—Aptiva and NetVista

After starting out as a small-scale experiment back in 1981, the IBM Personal Computer has now grown into several complete families of personal computers. The families (also called brands) that make up IBM's personal computer line are the IBM Aptiva, Personal Computer (PC), NetVista, Netfinity/xSeries, ThinkPad/WorkPad, and IntelliStation families, and finally IBM's Options brand of products, which are specially designed to support IBM's entire line of PC products. Each family is designed to suit the needs and buying habits of specific user communities (with some overlap between the families).

The Aptiva family is designed for use by individuals in very small businesses and at home. It currently consists of two series (E and the S), of different models, all with standard multimedia capabilities. Figure 2.3 shows a member of the Aptiva S family. The focus is on affordability, convenience, and ease of use. Yet, they also offer the latest in speed and technology. Unlike most of IBM's other PC families, Aptiva computers are offered only through a few select retailers and directly from IBM rather than through computer dealers or IBM

Figure 2.3. A member of IBM's Aptiva S Series.

marketing representatives. Because Aptivas are primarily for the individual and home market, they are not intended (or supported) for use in complex local area networks. PC families designed for use in complex networks undergo additional and extensive testing in various network environments, which adds costs consumers do not require. However, Aptivas do come with fax/modems and communications software that allow for everything from Internet access to telephone answering machine functions. Some models may also be supported in a small home network using approved network adapters. The new Aptivas, based on Intel's Pentium III and AMD's Athlon microprocessors, have the Windows 2000 operating system and several basic application programs pre-installed.

In 2000 IBM introduced a new line of desktop products, codenamed EoN for "Edge of the Network." This line of products is branded as IBM's new NetVista family of computers, which now expand IBM's PC evolution and help bring more users to the edge of the network. IBM NetVista constitutes a new product line of desktops and mobile systems under a single brand. This line will be closely tied to IBM's pervasive computing strategy. IBM may soon include a "Wearable PC" like the 13-ounce prototype that Olympus Optical Co. and IBM's Japanese unit unveiled in November. The Wearable PC has a tiny screen that flips out from a headset to cover one eye, projecting the image of a much larger monitor. We expect the NetVista brand name to eventually encompass all of IBM's line of commercial desktop and thin client systems in the future, similar to the transition we are seeing with IBM's PC server line, now called the @server xSeries.

The IBM Personal Computer (PC) brand and NetVista is also known under the umbrella name of Client Systems, denoting systems that can attach to a server over a network. This also means that the systems are network certified and supported in a network environment. The new IBM NetVista family of computers provide the ultimate connectivity in a stylish, space-saving designs for either home or office. IBM has introduced three design points of the NetVista product line, the all-in-one, legacy-free, and thin client. Each of these designs provides a wide range of function depending on the requirements of the users. IBM's commercial systems also provide many features that help businesses manage and protect their PC assets. The IBM Personal Computer family and NetVista family (Figure 2.4) covers a wide range of performance, features, and functions. There are IBM PC models based on the full range of Intel Pentium microprocessors and Voice Talent incorporating both ISA (Industry Standard Architecture) and PCI (Peripheral Component Interconnect) expansion buses.

The new IBM NetVista Family of computers is designed for simplicity. As mentioned earlier, IBM has introduced three series of NetVista products, the NetVista all-in-one, the NetVista legacy-free, and the NetVista Thin Client. They are designed with fewer cables and smaller sizes, which makes them easier to carry and set up. New portable drives, keyboards, and "Access IBM" buttons make them easier to use. The NetVista Family also has new networking and security features to make doing e-business easier. These new computers allow users to easily transfer data between computers with an option called the IBM Portable Drive Bay 2000. This new option allows you to reduce the number of hard drives or CD-RW drives with a single, swappable drive that works in both IBM ThinkPad notebook computers and NetVista desktop computers. NetVista also features an embedded security chip, available on select models of the legacy-free NetVista S40, which provides 256- bit encryption for extremely secure network and Internet transactions. The latest PC 300GL and PC 300PL systems now include up to a 933 MHz Pentium III processors with integrated cache and high-performance AGP graphics adapters.

Figure 2.4. IBM PC and Netvista families.

Meet the Server Families—xServer and Netfinity

The latest line of IBM Netfinity and xServers (Figure 2.5) covers a wide range of performance, features, and functions. (Note: All new enhanced models of the current Netfinity line will be part of the IBM @server xSeries brand which is replacing the current IBM Netfinity name). There are IBM Netfinity and xSeries server models based on a broad range of microprocessors extending from a single 600 MHz Pentium III processor to systems with as many as eight Symmetric MultiProcessing (SMP) Pentium III Xeon processors sharing the same PC Server. Industry Standard Architecture (ISA), Enhanced Industry

Figure 2.5. IBM Netfinity and @server xSeries.

Standard Architecture (EISA), and Peripheral Component Interconnect (PCI) products are offered in the IBM PC server family. All of IBM's PC servers come with an array of software including Lotus Domino Server software, Netfinity Manager, and IBM Server Guide.

IBM decided to provide manageability solutions based on industry standards for systems management. IBM's Universal Manageability (UM) initiative has been designed and developed to help streamline and automate management and support tasks such as asset deployment and tracking through leading-edge, standards-based tools. Second, IBM chose to provide products with proven, reliable technology while helping reduce the total cost of ownership. This commitment to technology leadership is expressed in IBM's X-architecture, which takes the best capabilities from larger IBM systems and adapts them into a framework that will integrate with a wide range of industry-standard, customer-chosen management and operating systems. Finally, IBM's strategy is to provide smooth integration with leading enterprise and workgroup management tools for a comprehensive solution that fits with your existing assets and grows as your business grows. IBM's Systems Management strategy supports a variety of management solutions that integrate smoothly with Tivoli Management Software, Computer Associates Unicenter TNG, Microsoft System Management Server (SMS), Intel LANDesk Management Suite, and others.

The main building blocks of Netfinity manageability are the server hardware and its instrumentation, including the Advanced System Management Processor, server deployment with ServerGuide and LANClient Control Manager (LCCM), and systems management software with Netfinity Director and Netfinity Manager. These building blocks help you deploy and install your hardware, physically manage your operations and assets, and provide remote support and maintenance.

IBM's Netfinity servers, with advanced local and remote management capabilities, provide that management, no matter the size of your networked business. Some models provide benefits such as warning when the ECC memory error threshold is being reached, Predictive Failure Analysis (PFA) for rapid identification of a failing component, automatic server restart, and IBM's Light-Path Diagnostics technology, which directs you to the location of a failed component within your server.

Meet the Notebook Family—Thinkpad

The IBM ThinkPad family (Figure 2.6) of computers is designed to be used both in and out of the office environment. Their key features are small size, lightweight, and battery power. All ThinkPad computers have built-in color displays. Some models are capable of recognizing your handwriting; others are capable of recording and playing back speech and music. The power and flexibility of these systems combined with the available optional features allow a single system to satisfy all computing needs of a traveling professional. The IBM WorkPad series of pocket-sized and extremely small notebook computers provides mobile individuals with a powerful extension to their desktop or laptop computers. These PC companions are more than just a personal organizer. They provide instant portable access to address books, a calendar, a memo pad, to-do lists, and downloaded e-mail.

IBM's ThinkPad family is now divided into three major series of notebook computers:

1. The ThinkPad ASeries consists of notebooks that are considered high-performance desktop and value desktop alternatives.

2. The ThinkPad TSeries consists of thin, light, high-performance notebooks that are an ideal balance of performance and portability for the traveler.

3. The ThinkPad iSeries consists of notebooks that are Internet optimized for individuals and tailored for personal productivity and small-business users.

IBM has simplified its ThinkPad product lineup and changed the naming scheme to connote the experience of the product. An A in the model number indicates that the computer is an alternative to a desktop computer; a T indicates it is a "thin-and-light" notebook. The ThinkPad 390 models are transitioning to the new ThinkPad A20m. Likewise, the ThinkPad 770 models are transitioning to the high-performance ThinkPad A20p, and the ThinkPad 600 is transitioning to the new ThinkPad T20. In addition to these three series, we will also discuss the ThinkPad 240X ultralight notebook and ThinkPad 570E ultraportable notebook.

Figure 2.6. IBM ThinkPad Family.

Consistent with IBM's EoN (Edge-of-Network) strategy, to simplify the computing experience for end-users and IT managers, IBM's ThinkPad continues to lead the way in delivering enhancements, innovations, and solutions that have shaped and defined the mobile computing category. The latest innovative enhancements include Titanium composite covers, which provide increased strength for protection. Titanium has been used for aerospace, orthopedics, and sporting equipment because of its high strength and low density. Titanium has natural dampening effect on vibrations and shocks. The new ThinkPad A20p and T20 come with titanium composite material as part of a carbon fiber reinforced plastic cover, adding strength. Titanium composite carbon fiber-reinforced plastic has three times the strength of ABS plastic. The use of titanium composite has helped IBM create some of the industry's thinnest and lightest systems with large displays (up to 15 inches).

Meet Some Other Family Members

There are several other more specialized members of the PC Heritage club. These are described below.

The IBM IntelliStation, which is also called the professional workstation (PWS) family of computers, is intended for the business professional who requires very high-end workstation performance to run graphically and compute intense 32-bit applications such as Computer-Aided Design (CAD) and statistical modeling. The IntelliStation bridges the gap between the traditional UNIX/RISC workstation and the PC by using high-end Intel-based processors running Microsoft's Windows NT.

The IBM Thin Client family is represented by IBM's new NetVista Network Stations, which are designed to replace Non-Programmable Terminals (NPTs) that connect to servers and mainframes. The IBM Network Station with its PowerPC Microprocessor is marketed through the IBM PC Company dealer channel. It provides users with a lower-cost access to the network than traditional PCs, but with many popular PC features such as SVGA graphics and mouse support that are lacking in a non-programmable terminal. The IBM Network Station software (sold separately) includes 3270, 5250, VTXXX, ASCII, and X-Server terminal emulation to give users access to their existing business applications on existing servers, including PC and UNIX servers, AS/400, RS6000, and S/390. The term thin client refers to PCs that are much smaller in size with less expansion capabilities.

Also worth mentioning is IBM's industrial computer line, which is intended for nonoffice environments. These PC-compatible systems are designed and packaged so that they can withstand harsher environments (e.g., higher temperatures, particulates, power surges, shock, vibration, and longer power-on hours) than mainstream personal computers.

Finally, the Options by IBM brand of products are designed and tested to provide accessories, upgrades, and monitors for all IBM PC lines. Options include: memory, storage, modems, networking adapters, docking stations/port replicators, batteries, power adapters, security cards, monitors, printers, scanners, keyboards, and mice.

Storage Area Networks

In February 1999 IBM announced details of its Storage Area Network (SAN) initiative and introduced a series of high-end SAN-related products. This initiative is designed to help customers manage, track, and more easily share the ever-increasing volume of data being created by e-business applications. SAN technology can lead to lower total cost of ownership by allowing storage resources to be consolidated and shared by several servers.

The ability to manage resources and share information has become crucial to many businesses today. Among the reasons are the growth of data-intensive applications such as data warehousing, data mining, and enterprise resource planning. Add to this the increasing presence of the Internet in commerce, and the need for companies to be open for business 24 hours a day, 7 days a week in multiple time zones, and—nearly around-the-clock access to business data is obvious. In this environment, data storage is rapidly becoming a central component of corporate technology strategies in the network.

SANs offer an open architecture that allows customers freedom of choice in deploying data access and data sharing capabilities across the enterprise, consolidation of servers and storage, increased data availability, centralized storage management, the ability to back up and migrate data without affecting enterprise network performance, the increased reliability offered by clustering technology, and the security and protection of data in the event of disaster or intrusions.

The SAN is the next generation in the evolution of enterprise storage solutions. Its development has become necessary as a result of worldwide customer requirements for data storage and processing around the clock in multiple time zones—storage and processing that are reliable, powerful, secure, and separate from the enterprise LAN.

IBM's @server SAN components and solutions are among the leading products in the industry. IBM brings decades of experience and expertise in mainframe technology to the Intel processor-based environment with their Netfinity/xSeries family of servers and options by IBM's broad portfolio of storage products. Both Netfinity/xSeries servers and Options by IBM installed on them are covered by IBM's limited, three-year on-site warranty, which provides hardware problem determination on-site, as well as remotely, with IBM's latest technology and tools.

IBM also provides the software management tools that help you fully exploit the value of a SAN in your business and make your business intelligence work for you. And the IBM ServerProven Program on Netfinity gives businesses the confidence to implement robust SAN solutions tested and optimized for Netfinity/xSeries systems in industry-standard, heterogeneous environments.

Now let's examine today's PCs by taking a closer look at some of the PC's different components.

Hardware Architecture

There are many elements that together provide the functions and performance of a computer. The rest of this chapter provides a closer look at the following elements of IBM's personal computers:

- Microprocessors

- Memory

- Disk storage

Microprocessors and Memory

Although there are many electronic circuits in personal computers, two key elements contribute the most to the systems' capabilities and performance. These are the microprocessor and the RAM (Random Access Memory, called the memory). The microprocessor and memory, along with other circuits, reside on a circuit board called the system board in most personal computers. In some, however, such as the Netfinity 5600 and 7600 servers, this circuitry is packaged on a processor card installed in a special slot or shuttle on the system board.

Microprocessor Basics

The microprocessor typically is the most important item in a computer system because it executes the instructions that make up a computer program, acts as the control center for information flow inside the computer, and performs calculations on the data. It is a single computer chip containing many thousands (or even millions) of microscopic circuits that work together to execute computer programs.

The microprocessor does the data manipulation or thinking necessary to perform tasks for the user.

The microprocessor is the central processing unit (CPU) of the computer. It is the place where most of the control and computing functions occur. All operating system and application program instructions are executed here. Most information passes through it, whether that information is a keyboard stroke, data from a disk, or information from a communication network.

The processor needs data and instructions for each processing operation that it performs. Data and instructions are loaded from memory into data-storage locations, known as registers, in the processor. Registers are also used to store the information that results from each processing operation until the data is transferred to memory. The microprocessor is packaged as an integrated circuit that contains one or more Arithmetic Logic Units (ALUs, or execution units), a floating-point unit, an on-board cache, registers for holding instructions and data, and control circuitry. This circuitry is used to perform the binary mathematics electrically inside the microprocessor.

A fundamental characteristic of all microprocessors is the rate at which they perform operations. This characteristic is called the clock rate and is measured in millions of cycles per second, or megahertz (MHz). The maximum clock rate of a microprocessor is determined by how fast the internal logic of the chip can be switched. As silicon fabrication processes are improved, the integrated devices on the chip become smaller and can be switched faster. Thus, the clock speed can be increased.

Multiprocessing

The speed of the microprocessor has a significant effect on a computer's performance. The internal structure (or architecture) of the microprocessor also determines the inherent capabilities of the personal computer in which it is used. Another way to increase the performance of the computer is through the use of multiple processors in a system. This is called multiprocessing. The two main types of multiprocessing are asymmetric and symmetric. In asymmetric (or loosely-coupled) processing, the CPUs are dedicated to specific tasks, so a CPU can be idle if a specific task is not needed. Asymmetric processing is no longer commonly used in the PC environment. In symmetric (tightly-coupled) processing, each CPU is available for any process task. An SMP (symmetric multiprocessing) system enhances performance by allowing a computer's whole workload to be distributed among all the CPUs. Additional CPUs act like all the others in processing tasks or threads of execution.

As there is overhead in managing additional processors, the system performance gain will be less than 100 percent for each processor. The performance gain is dependent on the operating system and type of application used. An operating system must support SMP. Applications also need to be designed for SMP (i.e., multithreaded) to realize the full potential of SMP.

IBM's new PC servers and IntelliStation PCs have support for SMP. For example, the Netfinity 5500 server supports dual Pentium III Xeon processors, and the new Netfinity 8500 supports as many as eight processors.

Intel Microprocessors

Since the beginning of the PC, IBM has continued to make computers based on Intel's line of CISC microprocessors. Figure 2.7 shows a history of the generations of Intel's processors. Although IBM has manufactured some number of their own microprocessors, the majority of IBM's PC models have used Intel processors. IBM PCs have evolved from Intel's 8088, 8086, 286, 386, and 486 to today's Pentium and Pentium III Xeon microprocessor architectures.

In 1999, Intel introduced the new Pentium III Xeon processor, which targets Intel's offerings to the workstation and server market segments, providing additional performance for e-commerce applications and advanced business computing. These new processors incorporate the Pentium III processor's 70 SIMD instructions, which enhance multimedia and streaming video applications. The Pentium III Xeon processor's advance cache technology speeds information from the system bus to the processor, significantly boosting performance. With speeds up to 933 MHz, Intel Pentium III Xeon processors are specifically designed to meet the demanding scalability and reliability requirements of mainstream and high-end Netfinity servers and IntelliStation workstations with multiprocessor configurations.

Introduction Year	Internal Processor	Clock	Bus Width	Number of Transistors	Addressable Memory
1971	4004	108KHz	4 bits	2,300	640 bytes
1972	8008	108KHz	8 bits	3,500	16K
1974	8080	2 MHz	8 bits	6,000	64K
1978	8086	5 MHz	16 bits	29,000	1 MB
1979	8088	5 MHz	16 bits	29,000	1 MB
1982	80286	8 MHz	16 bits	134,000	16 MB
1985	80386 DX	16 MHz	32 bits	275,000	4 GB
1989	80486 DX	25 MHz	32 bits	1,200,000	4 GB
1993	Pentium	60 MHz	32 bits	3.2 million	4 GB
1995	Pentium Pro	150 MHz	64 bits	5.5 million	4 GB
1997	Pentium MMX	166 MHz	32 bits	4.5 million	4 GB
1997	Pentium II	233 MHz	64 bits	7.5 million	64 GB
1998	Celeron	233 MHz	64 bits	7.5 million	64 GB
1999	Pentium III	450 MHz	64 bits	10 million	64 GB

Figure 2.7. History of major Intel processor introductions used in computers. (Not all variations are listed.)

The features of the Pentium III Xeon processor eliminate the key roadblocks that previously limited performance on the most demanding IntelliStation workstation or Netfinity server. The processor core speed executes instructions quickly, while dynamic execution and smooth multiprocessing allow work to be performed in parallel. Intel's full-speed L2 cache, large cache sizes, and 133 MHz system bus reduce memory latency, facilitating the movement of data through the processor and I/O devices.

Intel's latest line of IA-64 processors was announced in 2000 and named the Intel Itanium processor. Previously known by the code name Merced, the Itanium processor employs a 64-bit architecture and enhanced instruction handling to greatly increase the performance of demanding e-business, visualization, computation, and multimedia operations. IBM IntelliStation workstations and Netfinity servers, optimized to take advantage of the Intel IA-64 architecture and Itanium 64-bit processors, are currently in development. These new high-performance, 64-bit-based workstations and servers will benefit customers working with large models and/or data sets in fields such as engineering, scientific analysis, simulations, and digital creation.

Memory

The memory is also a very important part of a computer. Memory is the set of electronic chips that provide a workspace for the microprocessor. The memory holds the information being used by the microprocessor. This memory, as noted earlier, is called RAM (Random Access Memory) because it can store and retrieve any piece of information independently of the sequential order in which it was originally stored. The smallest piece of information that can be stored in memory is called a bit. These bits are grouped into bytes (8 bits), words (16 bits), and double words (32 bits) to form the computer's representation of numbers, letters of the alphabet, and instructions in a program.

The amount of memory in IBM Personal Computers ranges from 64 MB (IBM ThinkPad Model 240) to a maximum of 16 GB (Netfinity 8500 Server). As memory increases, so do the chances of having a memory failure, which can cause the computer system to deliver erroneous information or abruptly halt the system altogether. To combat this problem, the IBM Personal Computers that can be configured with the largest memories, including the IBM Netfinity Server systems, employ schemes to detect and correct memory defects, thus protecting the integrity of the information stored in the computer system's main memory. These schemes, called Error Checking and Correcting (ECC), can detect both single-and double-bit errors and can correct single-bit errors.

It is important to mention three other types of memory in personal computers: Read-Only Memory (ROM), Flash Erasable Programmable Read-Only Memory (flash EPROM), and Complementary Metal Oxide Semiconductor (CMOS) memory. Each PC contains some amount of ROM, which permanently stores some special housekeeping programs used to manage the internal operation of the computer. The memory is called ROM because information it contains cannot be altered or written to, it can only be read. The information stored in ROM is preserved even when the computer is turned off. In many of the newer PCs, flash EPROM is used to store the same housekeep-

of the newer PCs, flash EPROM is used to store the same housekeeping programs that traditionally were stored in standard ROM. As the name implies, the flash EPROM is a read-only memory that can be erased and reprogrammed using a special technique. Like standard ROM memory, the information is preserved even when the computer is turned off. However, since the flash EPROM can be altered, the information can be loaded into the EPROM from a diskette, using the utility software that comes with the system. This provides an easy way to correct possible errors once you have purchased the system or to add enhanced function to upgrade performance or function.

CMOS memory gets its name from the transistor technology used to build the memory. The information in CMOS memory, unlike the information in ROM, can be altered at any time. The low power consumption inherent in CMOS technology allows the internal battery to preserve the information stored in CMOS memory even when the computer is turned off. The CMOS memory is used to store system configuration and diagnostic information. The CMOS memory chip also has circuitry that automatically keeps track of the current time of day and date. This time and date information is available for use by an application program and is used by operating systems to track when disk files were created, when files were last modified, and so on.

Disk Storage

Disk storage, commonly used in personal computers, provides a relatively inexpensive way to store computer data and programs. The information stored on disk can be modified easily or kept unchanged over long periods of time as an archive. The information remains intact whether the computer is turned on or off. Thus, disk storage is said to be nonvolatile. All personal computers (except for medialess workstations) use two types of magnetic disk storage: diskettes and fixed disks.

The other type of disk storage available in personal computers today is called Optical Disk Storage, which is growing in importance as multimedia applications become more prevalent. There are several types of optical disk storage available for PCs. Next, we look at the diskette, fixed-disk, and optical storage commonly used with personal computers.

Diskettes

Diskettes are portable magnetic storage media that can be used to record and later retrieve computer information via a diskette drive. One of the primary functions of a diskette is to provide portable disk storage, allowing for the transfer of programs and data between computers. All IBM Personal Computers use 3.5-inch diskettes as opposed to the 5.25-inch diskettes used by earlier PCs. These diskette types are compared in Figure 2.8. The outer case of the 5.25-inch diskettes is flexible and does not completely cover the sensitive magnetic material actually containing the information. The 3.5-inch diskette has a rigid outer case that completely encloses the magnetic material. A sliding metal cover, which protects the magnetic material, is retracted only while the diskette is inside the diskette drive. For these reasons, the 3.5-inch diskettes are less susceptible to damage that may result during normal handling. Further, the 3.5-inch diskettes are small enough to fit conveniently into a pocket or purse. The write-protect switch (not visible) in the lower-left corner on the back of the diskette allows you to prevent the accidental overwriting of information. When the switch is positioned so that the square hole in the lower-left corner is open, the diskette is write-protected. When

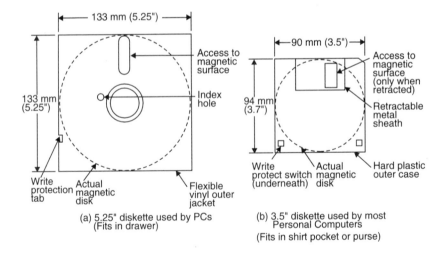

Figure 2.8. The 5.25-inch and 3.5-inch diskette.

the switch is blocking the square hole, information can be written to the diskette. Some diskettes, such as the reference diskette, do not have this switch and are therefore permanently write-protected.

Fixed Disks

Another kind of disk storage used with IBM Personal Computers is called a fixed disk (or simply a disk). Fixed disks are fast high-capacity magnetic storage devices commonly used in most personal computers as well as in the largest computer systems. They consist of a drive mechanism with permanently installed metallic disks coated with a magnetic material. An activity light on your PC is usually provided and is illuminated when a fixed disk is being accessed. The circuitry that controls these fixed disks is packaged with the fixed disk drive itself (called an integrated controller), on the system board, or on a separate feature card.

Optical Disk Storage

Almost a necessity for today's PC is an optical disk drive that can at least read a CD-ROM disk (Compact Disk-Read Only Memory). There are several optical drives that do this and more. IBM has PC models with CD-ROM, Rewritable CD, and DVD (Digital Video Disc) drives that are all capable of reading CD-ROM disks. CD-ROM disks use the same technique to store information as audio compact disks. Rather than using magnetics, CD-ROM systems use optical techniques to achieve their much higher density. A single disk used in a CD-ROM drive can hold about 600 MB of information. That is enough storage to hold over 300,000 sheets of computer output, or a stack over 90 feet high. CD-ROM drives are read-only. That is, personal computer users can view the information but they can't change it.

Rewritable CD drives produce a CD that can be read by a CD-ROM drive as well, using special rewritable CD disks. DVD drives provide the largest amount of optical storage with more than four times the storage of CD-ROMs that also allow the user to play today's DVD movies. The primary use of CD-ROM storage is to distribute large amounts of information in a convenient package. Potential uses for CD-ROM include distribution of program libraries, financial reports, operations manuals, phone directories, or any large (and relatively stable) database, as well as, backing up large amounts data when using rewritable CD drives.

The extremely high storage capacity of CD-ROMs can be attributed to the technique used to store the information. When the CD-ROM is first recorded, a laser beam is used to burn tiny patterns on the reflective surface of an optical disk according to industry standards. Later, by bouncing the low-power laser beam in the CD-ROM drive off the optical disk's surface, a series of mirrors and sensors can read back the information that was burned into the disk. DVD-ROMs are similar but use additional optical layers to achieve a much higher storage capacity. Although this optical technology lends itself quite well to the information distribution applications mentioned earlier, their limited speed (as compared to fixed disks) and much slower ability to record information (when using rewritable drives) preclude using CD-ROM and DVD-ROM disks as normal fixed-disk storage.

PC Software

Software is like a publication. Newspapers are a category of publication; annual reports, novels, and Who's Who directories are some other categories of publications. These different categories fill very different needs. The same situation exists with software. The different categories of software are diverse in function and purpose. In this section you learn how the various unique and highly specialized programs interact, through descending levels, to communicate with the hardware in your CPU.

Types of Software—A Model

The basic categories of real software used with all personal computers to perform useful work can be understood through the simple software model in Figure 2.9. There are three basic categories, or software layers, commonly used with PCs: the application program layer, the operating system layer, and the Basic Input/Output System

(BIOS) layer. Although each software layer performs a completely different job, all three work closely together to perform useful work for the user. Some special-purpose programs do not fit neatly into any of the three categories, but the majority of the software commonly used to perform business tasks does. Software programs for the various IBM families are further discussed in later chapters.

Application Programs

The top software layer in the software model is the application program layer, highlighted in Figure 2.10. The programs in this layer apply personal computers to specific tasks such as word processing and communications. Thus, they are called application programs. They actually perform the task the user purchased the computer for, while the other two layers play important support roles.

The User's View arrows in Figure 2.10 indicate that the user usually interacts with the application program layer and less frequently interacts with the operating system. By working closely with the other software layers, the application program processes the various key-

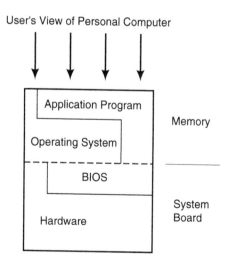

Figure 2.9. Conceptual software model of the basic software structure of Personal Computers. The three layers of the software model work together to perform useful work for the user.

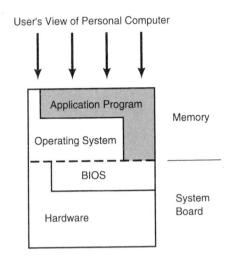

Figure 2.10. The application program software layer, highlighted in the software model above, defines the particular task the computer is performing for the user.

strokes made by the user and responds by displaying information on the computer's display or some other output device.

As we see later in this chapter, newer personal computers can execute most of the programs written for the original IBM PC. This allows personal computer users to capitalize on the thousands of application programs originally developed for IBM PCs and compatibles. Common functions that application programs perform in the business environment are accounting, financial modeling, word processing, database management, communications, and computer graphics. There is an application program that can help the user with just about anything he or she wishes to do.

Operating Systems

The next layer in our software model, called the operating system, is highlighted in Figure 2.11. The operating system must manage the hardware resources of the computer system and perform tasks under the control of application programs and keyboard/mouse/touch-screen input from the user. The application program can rely on the operating system to perform many of the detailed housekeeping tasks associated with the internal workings of the computer. Thus, the operating system is said to provide the environment in which application programs execute. Operating systems also accept input directly from the user to perform such tasks as formatting diskettes and clearing the screen.

BIOS

The third and final layer of software in our software model is the BIOS layer, highlighted in Figure 2.12. BIOS is a set of specialized programs that, unlike application programs or operating systems, are used only by other programs. BIOS never interacts directly with the user and exists only to help application programs and operating systems perform tasks. In fact, the user never even knows it is there. BIOS assists the operating system and application programs in performing tasks directly involving details of the computer hardware. BIOS also shields a computer program from the hardware specifics of computers, allowing these specifics to evolve as new computers are designed without causing software compatibility problems.

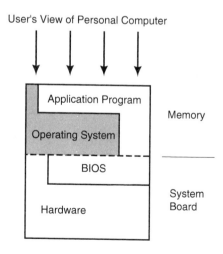

Figure 2.11. The operating system software layer, highlighted in the software model above, provides the environment in which the application program(s) run.

Unlike operating systems or application programs that must be loaded into memory from disk, BIOS is permanently stored in the Read-Only Memory (ROM) chips within the personal computer along with the POST program. Many of the newer personal computer models store a large portion of the BIOS in flash memory, which can easily be updated using special information provided on the reference diskette.

Most personal computers have both a compatibility BIOS and an advanced BIOS. The compatibility BIOS is provided to preserve software compatibility with PCs. This same type of BIOS was supplied with all earlier PC computers. The advanced BIOS is a completely independent set of programs, also stored in the personal computer's ROM (or flash memory). Advanced BIOS provides a more-advanced set of programming tools used by operating system programmers and provides specific support for the multi-application environment.

Operating Systems

Few topics in the personal computer area create more confusion and apprehension than the operating system. Never before has the user

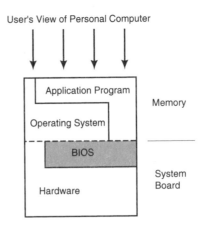

Figure 2.12. The BIOS software layer, highlighted in the software model above, directly controls the hardware elements of Personal Computers and shields application programs and operating systems from the hardware details.

had more operating system alternatives. This section removes some of the mystery associated with operating systems used on IBM Personal Computers. It is designed to familiarize you with operating system topics, such as multi-application and extended memory, and how these concepts apply to the business environment. It also discusses specific operating system products for IBM Personal Computers.

The Disk Operating System (DOS)

The PC disk operating system, commonly called DOS, was the operating system originally offered for the IBM Personal Computer. It was primarily designed to provide a single-application, single-user environment—whereas today's operating systems (such as Microsoft's Windows, covered later in the chapter) provide PCs with a multi-application and multi-tasking environment.

DOS provides an IBM PC-compatible, single-application environment. It consists of a set of programs designed to perform many diverse hardware housekeeping tasks under the control of either the user or an application program. As the name DOS implies, many of these housekeeping tasks deal with the fixed disks in personal computers. Other tasks performed by DOS include starting application programs, setting the computer's date and time, sending information to a printer, and managing files.

While the DOS operating system is still provided as a back-up operating system with many personal computers today, advancements in the microprocessor and basic PC architecture have given way to more advanced operating system structures.

Advanced Operating Systems

The full capabilities of IBM Personal Computers are not unleashed unless the operating system fully exploits the advanced features offered by the ever-increasing advancements in microprocessor technology. The original IBM PC design needed an architected path to overcome an early 640-KB memory limitation. Thus, there was a need for a more advanced operating systems architecture.

In addition, there are other advantages offered by advanced operating systems. For example, the Virtual 8086 mode of the earlier 386/486 Intel family of microprocessors allowed personal computers to behave as if there were several independent computers cooperating to perform work for one user.

There are several different operating system environments that more fully exploit the advanced capabilities of the microprocessors used in IBM Personal Computers. Now let's take a closer look at the advanced operating system alternatives.

Windows

The Windows program, developed by Microsoft Corp., was used to extend the basic DOS functions in the area of multi-application and maximum memory size. The 3.1 version of Windows included additional enhancements in the areas of performance, file management, font capability, reliability, and network integration. Windows helped overcome the 640-KB memory limit of the original IBM PC, which is still with us in today's DOS environment for the sake of compatibility. It was important to somehow overcome this 640-KB limit, because as you begin to load multiple application programs into memory, you quickly run out of space in the 640-KB area.

In the area of multi-applications, Windows allows the user to start up and run more than one application program at a time (i.e., multi-application support). To manage these applications, Windows subdivides the display screen into multiple rectangular areas called windows. Each application program then resides in its own window to facilitate quick and convenient switching from one application to another (i.e., program switching). A mouse is used to interact with Windows for actions such as selecting which window is the active window, starting programs, resizing windows, moving windows around on the screen, and so on. Small images called icons are drawn on the display to indicate that application programs are loaded but not currently shown in a window. This type of user interface based on icons, windows, and so on, is called a graphical user interface (GUI). Some application programs can remain active (in the background) while you are interacting with another (in the foreground). However, because Windows 3.1

worked in conjunction with DOS (a non-multi-application operating system), there were limitations to the multi-application environment provided by the DOS/Windows environment.

Windows 98

Microsoft's Windows 98 operating system is the successor to the Windows 95 operating system. Through the integration of Microsoft's key Internet Explorer technologies to unify and simplify the desktop, Windows 98 makes it easier for users to find and navigate to information. Help features have been simplified with the addition of 15 new troubleshooting wizards and Web-based help. Windows 98 provides support for new hardware devices including native support for Universal Serial Bus (USB), DVD (digital video disc), and television broadcast capabilities, as well as support for the latest graphics, sound, and multimedia technologies. Windows 98 also features an improved version of the File Allocation Table (FAT) file system, called FAT32. FAT32 helps give you more hard-drive space by more-efficiently using space on large disks. A graphical conversion utility lets you quickly and safely convert a hard drive to FAT32.

Windows 98 also shuts down and launches applications faster than Windows 95. If you have a system with the new Advanced Configuration and Power Interface (ACPI) fast-boot BIOS support, Windows 98 will enable you to boot your system faster. A new system file checker is provided to help you keep track of critical files that make your computer run. If these files are moved or changed, system file checker provides an easy way to restore these files. After file changes are detected, it offers you several courses of action. Windows 98 adds support for up to nine multiple monitors and/or multiple graphics adapters on a single PC. Multiple displays can let you spread out and interact more easily between documents and applications. Finally, Microsoft Windows 98 provides a suite of tools for Internet communication, including Outlook Express, an e-mail and news-reading; Microsoft NetMeeting, for Internet conferencing; Personal Web Server (for publishing Web pages); Microsoft FrontPad HTML editor; and Microsoft NetShow multimedia services.

Windows 2000

The Microsoft Windows 2000 operating system arrived in the year 2000 as the successor to the Windows 98 and Windows NT operating systems. Windows NT (discussed in more detail later on) is Microsoft's operating system for business and server environments. Windows 2000 is, in fact, a complete product line of operating systems, spanning a full-range of computing needs, from the desktop to high-end clustered servers. For the desktop and mobile computer user Windows 2000 Professional replaces Windows 98 and for the server environment Windows 2000 Server operating systems replace Windows NT 4.0 Server.

Windows 2000 Professional for the client provides improved support for the next-generation of hardware and streamlines the familiar Windows 98 interface by reducing desktop clutter and simplifying the Start menu. In addition to removing unnecessary desktop items, Windows 2000 Professional introduces personalized menus, with a new smart feature that adapts the Start menu to the way you work by showing you the applications you typically use most often. Windows 2000 Professional also builds on the reliability strengths of Windows NT. For example, the operating system detects, identifies, and prevents memory leaks that can develop over time and can cause your system to be unstable.

The Windows 2000 Server operating systems are the next generation of the Windows NT Server series of operating systems. Windows 2000 Server series provide for a comprehensive Internet and user applications platform that builds on the strengths of the Windows NT Server 4.0 by providing increased reliability, availability, and scalability with enhanced end-to-end management features. At the core of Windows 2000 Server is a complete set of infrastructure services based on Microsoft's Active Directory service. The Active Directory simplifies management and provides a centralized way to manage users, groups, security services, and network resources. In addition, the Active Directory has a number of standard interfaces making it easy to operate with a variety of applications and devices.

The Windows 2000 Server family consists of three editions: Standard, Advanced, and Datacenter. The Standard edition is expected to be the most popular version for small to medium-sized businesses with a comprehensive set of Web and Internet services that allow organizations to take advantage of the latest Web technologies. Windows 2000 Server Standard edition also supports uniprocessor systems and 4-way symmetric multiprocessing (SMP) systems with up to 4 gigabytes (GB) of physical memory. The Advanced and Datacenter editions are designed to meet the needs of more advanced mission critical deployments in medium, large, and Internet Service Provider (ISP) organizations. For example, the Windows 2000 Datacenter Server is a specialized high-end version of Windows 2000 Server, that supports up to 32-way SMP and up to 64 GB of physical memory. Like Windows 2000 Advanced Server, it provides support for both clustering of multiple SMP servers and load balancing services as standard features.

OS/2 Warp Operating System

The IBM OS/2 Warp operating system allows a personal computer to offer its resources (fixed-disk storage, printers, etc.) to other personal computers in the LAN. It provides an application server foundation with integrated file and print sharing, backup and recovery, systems management, advanced printing, and Internet access. When a personal computer offers resources to others in a network, that computer is called a server. The computer system accessing those resources is called a requester or a client. The server would have OS/2 and the OS/2 Warp Server installed. The client can have DOS, Windows, or OS/2 Warp Client installed.

OS/2 Warp Server allows you to implement networked applications such as e-mail, Lotus Notes, and relational database systems. Or you can start with traditional file and print services and add more functions when you need them. As well as providing TCP/IP function, Warp Server can also be used as a Web server. The IBM Warp Server for e-business supports large, multi-server network environments with hundreds of users, and small installations with only a few users. Providing enhanced reliability, performance, capacity, and functionality, it supports many mission-critical applications simultaneously running on one server. While OS/2 Warp Server SMP has been optimized for four-CPU systems, it has support for up to 64-CPU systems (64-way SMP). Also, OS/2 Warp Server SMP includes improved high memory support that allows it to use larger amounts of virtual RAM. If you have an existing NetWare LAN, you can run OS/2 Warp Server concurrently and add such essential capabilities as Internet access, application services, and remote access.

Windows NT Server

Although Windows NT Workstation incorporates peer-to-peer networking as an integral part of the operating system, a separate product, Windows NT Server, offers significantly enhanced functions to implement advanced domain-administered networks. The capabilities of NT Server can be grouped into four basic categories: network management and administration, security and logon control, reliability, and client support. NT Server adds the concept of domains to the Windows environment. A domain is essentially a group of servers that can be managed as a group from a single system. This centralization allows user profiles and information to be stored in a single location, simplifying the management of large networks.

The Windows NT Server 5.0 is the latest version of NT Server and includes SMP support for multiprocessing and expanded Internet, intranet, and communications services. NT Server also incorporates support for RAID redundant array of inexpensive disks, which increases performance and reliability by spreading data across any array of disks and protects that data with a parity check. In addition, NT Server makes it easier to configure clients via directory replication. This feature lets a server automatically load files from a particular server directory into designated clients. Remote users are also supported through Remote Access Services (RAS).

JavaOS for Business

The JavaOS for Business operating system is a new operating system developed jointly by Sun Microsystems, Inc. and IBM. It was designed from the ground up to run Java applications in a centrally-managed, network-computing environment. With JavaOS for Business, servers can be connected to network computers and other thin clients such as kiosks, ticket machines, and remote terminals. The JavaOS for Business operating system was specifically designed to help simplify the management and remote administration of servers that host Java technology-based business applications for remote users, such as bank tellers, insurance claim processors, and travel agents.

Networks running JavaOS for Business software can provide various tools and applications for end users performing specialized tasks. Bank tellers, for example, need only a few applications to perform their jobs. JavaOS for Business software efficiently delivers these applications from the server to network computers, which often don't require devices such as hard disks or CD-ROMs. By providing only the operating system facilities necessary to support the Java platform, this new operating system eliminates the overhead required by other operating systems that support a variety of applications, hardware devices, and environments. In addition, the software also uses a layered architecture, which provides flexibility and ease of use, because each layer can be updated independently.

JavaOS for Business software is designed to give companies greater flexibility in implementing server-managed solutions because it is an open system based on industry standards. As a result, businesses can greatly reduce system administration costs while implementing the advantages of low-cost network computer systems.

Linux

The Linux operating system is a UNIX-like operating system that is an outgrowth of the Open Source community. Linux is fast becoming the operating system of choice for many new Internet companies and Web sites since it is essentially free and works dependably. The big difference between Linux and a proprietary network operating systems is that Linux is open-source, so it can be seen, used, modified, or augmented by anyone. You can download the code free from the Internet or buy a package of the operating system, tools, shells and utilities such as the Java 1.1.8 IBM Developer Kit for Linux. The IBM Developer Kit for Linux, Java Technology Edition, Version 1.1.8 is a development environment for companies who want to build and deploy high performance, Web-based, server applications on Intel architecture that conform to the Java 1.1 Core API. The Developer Kit for Linux contains IBM's Just-In-Time (JIT) compiling technology ported to the Linux environment and is compliant with Sun's Version 1.1.8 Java compatibility test. Linux is a well-suited operating system for a thin-client architecture running Java applications. While this UNIX spin-off is emerging as a viable operating system at the server level, its suitability for business desktops is still a matter of debate. IBM recently became the first vendor to offer Red Hat's Linux operating system as a certified operating system for a notebook computer, offering it on its ThinkPad.

Meet the NUMA-Q Family

The NUMA-Q Family of IBM Servers consists of two lines of server models that provide a wide range of performance and availability. The NUMA-Q 2000 (Figure 2.13) is a high end data center server, scalable to 64 processors with industry leading performance while the NUMA-Q 1000 (Figure 2.14) is a midrange UNIX server designed to offer very competitive price/performance.

The NUMA-Q 2000

The NUMA-Q 2000 series is built with Intel microprocessors so that organizations can gain the best performance and scalability available on Intel architecture-based enterprise server systems. These latest Intel processors incorporate Web and data-center-class features that are designed to support business-critical applications. Because the NUMA architecture virtually has no SMP backplane limits to scalability, NUMA-Q 2000 can meet the demands of increasing data volumes and user workloads. In addition the innovative interconnect technology, IQ-Link, enables high performance by cutting latencies to half those of the previous generation and providing cache coherency within each system node. Flexible memory configurations of one to 64 gigabytes per node provide optimal memory sizing to meet performance requirements.

The NUMA-Q 2000 model 410, for example, can provide a single server node using 4 to 64 or a two node cluster with 8 to 128 Intel Pentium III Xeon processors that run at 700 MHz speed with a processor L1 32KB and L2 512KB, 2 MB cache. Memory options for a single node NUMA-Q server provides from 1 to 64GB while a two node cluster provides from 2 to 128GB.

Figure 2.13. A member of the NUMA-Q 2000 family.

The NUMA-Q 2000 servers are adaptable and designed to meet IT requirements quickly as business models change. The 2000 servers provide for high availability and data-center-class manageability to meet the demands placed on enterprise servers by Web technologies and end user requirements for global, round-the-clock access to applications and services.

The NUMA-Q 1000

The NUMA-Q 1000 series is midrange single node server that supports a distributed computing environment or "virtual data center" as a departmental server and as a platform for midrange applica-

Figure 2.14. A member of the NUMA-Q 1000 family.

tions such as Web servers, data marts, and enterprise resource planning. The NUMA-Q 1000 is available in a four or eight-processor system, and offers many of the same data center features and benefits of the high-end NUMA-Q 2000 while also providing excellent price/performance. Through use of NUMA-Q architecture and Intel Pentium III Xeon processors, the high end NUMA-Q 1000 yields UNIX performance results similar to four- and eight-processor NUMA-Q 2000 configurations. For product line simplification reasons IBM recently discontinued the 1000 series as a 2000 series model can be configured with the same characteristics.

The NUMACenter

The NUMACenter (Figure 2.15) is a total network-centric solution offering that provides the technology to manage a consolidated data center composed of Web technologies, Online Transaction Processing (OLTP), and Business Intelligence (BI) applications joined together in a single, managed environment. NUMACenter includes NUMA-Q servers, operating systems, databases, systems management tools, integration services, and the expertise to integrate these components into a heterogeneous computing environment. Web and other networking technologies support OLTP and BI applications to form one cohesive environment. A NUMACenter solution can handle a consolidated data center's requirements with fewer resources, while increasing levels of service.

Since NUMACenter is a mixed-mode, multi-tier structure based on the Intel architecture and can scale to match UNIX and Windows NT capabilities, it allows Information Technology (IT) operations to deploy the operating system that makes the most sense for

Figure 2.15. A NUMACenter.

the application, and allocate hardware resources accordingly. NUMACenter enables simultaneous use of both UNIX and Windows NT on one system.

NUMA-Q Architecture

NUMA-Q architecture was designed to target the commercial data center computing environment. It is important to understand the commercial data center in order to appreciate fully the NUMA-Q architecture. Computer systems in these centers have several characteristics in common. They need to be highly available, highly reliable, capable of meeting ever-increasing performance demands, highly scalable, and easy to manage. The primary applications in today's data center computing environment fall into three major categories:

- OLTP refers to the day-to-day management of business functions using a relational database. An airline reservation application is an example of OLTP.

- Decision support systems (DSS) or BI refer to the extraction, analysis, and presentation of data from databases to enable business decision-making based on business operations. A parts usage and warranty repair analysis application used to determine a product's mean time to failure is a good example of a DSS.

- Collaboration refers to messaging, e-mail, document sharing or retrieval, and workflow. An Internet Web server like the one described in Chapter One is a good example of a business collaboration application that may run in a data center environment.

Prior to the advent of the NUMA architecture, OLTP, DSS, BI and collaboration systems designers had four architectural server options for their computing platforms:

- Small networked-servers

- Large Symmetric Multiprocessing (SMP) nodes

- Clustered SMP nodes

- MPP (Massively Parallel Processor) systems

Each architecture has characteristics that can be a help or be a hindrance, depending on the application requirements with respect to I/O, memory, processor, and connectivity. This makes the choice of hardware architecture largely dependent on the applications used.

Small networked-servers can be configured as a group of multiple small standalone servers connected over a network. It is true that a collection of networked servers can be successfully and economically applied to some problems such as a small World Wide Web service, or a digital library for presentations and documents in large corporations. However, the networked-servers model is not suitable for implementing large OLTP, BI, and collaboration applications. Another difficulty with implementing a vast network of small servers is management and availability.

SMP means that many processors and other resources run under one instance of the operating system. The processors are housed in the same server hardware system. Large single-node SMP systems are popular because they are ideally suited to large BI and OLTP applications. Data managed by an SMP system is centrally located. This allows users to share a pool of resources while making the SMP system easy to manage. SMP systems also provide a smooth migration path for sophisticated uniprocessor applications to high-performance multi-processor systems. One drawback for large single-node SMP systems is the potential architectural limit on the amount of I/O into and out of single-node SMP systems. As a business grows, BI and collaboration applications will continue to require increasing amounts of I/O. Another concern for large single-node SMP systems is that there are single points of failure, which can cause application interruptions.

In Clustered SMP nodes you have multiple instances of an application running on separate nodes under separate instances of an operating system, but sharing some storage devices and data. Clustered SMP nodes provide a solution to the latter problem by configuring the interconnection of single SMP systems into a cluster of nodes. Clustering can provide increased availability and enough performance on one or more nodes with access to common resources to completely replace the unplanned loss of another node. In the event of a single node outage, the other nodes continue to operate and may automatically assume the load of the failed node in a period of minutes. Clusters can also achieve far greater performance and scalability than a single SMP node because of the increase in I/O bandwidth, memory, and access to processors. Clustered SMP performance is still improving, especially with the advent of software that can take advantage of replicated memory technology such as IBM's Scalable Data Interconnect (SDI).

Massively Parallel Processor (MPP) systems provide for many unique instances of an operating system and applications, on separate nodes, usually without any shared resource, and communicating by passing messages via a high performance switch with a network. One major advantage of MPP architectures is the ability to connect hundreds of processor/memory cells or individual nodes with their own copy of the OS and application. However, the design of many MPP systems can also be a disadvantage when applications require a large amount of I/O or require many updates as with OLTP where the cumbersome messaging of MPP can become a bottleneck. The architecture of most MPP systems is a complex environment that is difficult to program in—thus limiting the range of applications that require those complex super-computer type calculations where an MPP system is a suitable choice. Today, the new NUMA-Q Architecture overcomes the architectural limitations of virtually all the current approaches to building enterprise-class computing systems for the data center environment.

In the process, two breakthrough technologies have been invented—the NUMA-Q architecture and the IQ-Link interconnect—that will have a great impact on system design for years to come. In simplest terms—a system based on the NUMA-Q architecture uses multiple four processor SMP building blocks, called "quads," each tied together with the new IQ-Link interconnect technology to form a single large computing complex. NUMA-Q architecture leverages the Intel 4x Pentium III Xeon processor SMP baseboard as a commodity building block for large systems. Intel's new Pentium III Xeon processor systems use newer Intel bus logic that allows for third-party control of the processor bus. Third-party control is the "hook" required to permit the joining of multiple quads together to form a larger system. In the quad CPUs, memory and I/O are uniquely arranged. The NUMA-Q design has essentially pulled memory apart and put pieces of it near each processor. I/O is also closer to each processor, yielding several advantages. The primary advantage is that for all memory and I/O accesses that can be satisfied inside the quad, there is no need to go out and use bandwidth on the interconnect between quads. In the NUMA-Q architecture, many of these accesses are handled at the quad level. When a memory access does go out on the IQ-Link interconnect, it happens quickly. The advantage of having memory and I/O in the quad near the processors is that the bus that links these together can operate independently of all the other quads until it makes a request that must be fulfilled outside the quad. The effective bus bandwidth of the system is now the summation of all the quads' 500 MB/sec buses, or 32 GB/sec for a 252-processor system. With two PCI buses in each quad, each rated at 133 MB/sec, half of this 32 GB/sec can be used for I/O.

The IQ-Link connection technology for linking multiple quads can be made memory-coherent (as in creating a single large SMP system from multiple quads), or the links can be used strictly for fast, low-latency message-passing (as in the case of networked-server or clusters architecture). These attributes are also those needed to tie clusters of large SMP servers together to maximize performance. In order for a group of quads to run as a single SMP system (a node), the interconnect creates a single large contiguous coherent view of memory out of the distributed pieces of physical memory found in each quad.

Because IQ-Link can provide this unified view of memory, with ranges of the address space parceled out to each quad, one instance of the OS and the applications simultaneously runs on all interconnected quads. The result is a very large, single-node SMP system that is the most suitable design for data center computing type applications. Now that we have a background on the NUMA-Q architecture, let's look at IBM's new NUMA-Q family.

NUMA-Q Software

The previous sections examined the various models of the IBM NUMA-Q family. Here we look at how you put that hardware to work—the all-important software.

Types of Software—A Conceptual Model

There are different categories of software, diverse in function and purpose. The basic categories of "real software" used in NUMA-Q systems can be understood through the model shown in Figure 2.16. There are three basic categories, or software layers, used in NUMA-Q systems: the application program layer, the operating system layer, and the device driver layer. Each software layer performs a completely different job, but all three work closely together to perform useful work for the user. Although some special-purpose programs do not fit neatly into any of these three categories, the majority of software does. Below is examination of each of the three layers in our software model.

Application Programs

The top software layer in the software model is the application program layer (highlighted in Figure 2.17). The programs in this layer "apply" the NUMA-Q system to a specific task (OLTP, BI, etc.) and

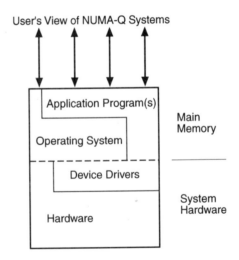

Figure 2.16. The three layers of the NUMA-Q system's basic software structure, shown in the conceptual software model above, work together to perform useful work for the user.

thus are called "application" programs. They actually perform the task for which the user purchased the computer while the other two layers play important support roles. A single NUMA-Q system might run one application program at a time, or it might run many application programs simultaneously.

The arrows in the figure indicate how users conceptually "see" the computer system. The user usually interacts with the application program layer and (less frequently) the operating system layer. By working closely with the other software layers, the application program processes the various keystrokes made by the user and responds by displaying information on the computer's display or some other output device. Many application programs written for other computers that run another variant of the UNIX operating system can be migrated to NUMA-Q systems by a software developer.

Operating Systems

The next layer in our software model is the operating system (highlighted in Figure 2.18). The operating system must manage the hard-

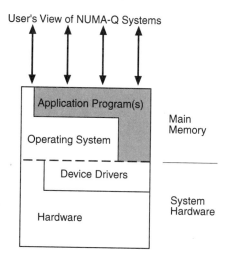

Figure 2.17. The application program software layer, highlighted in the software model above, is the application program that defines the particular task the computer is performing for the user.

ware resources of the computer system and perform tasks under the control of application program(s) and keyboard/mouse commands issued by the user. The application program can rely on the operating system to perform many of the detailed housekeeping tasks associated with the internal workings of the computer. Thus, the operating system is said to provide the environment in which application programs execute. The operating system layer also accepts commands directly from the user; for instance, it can copy files, change a user's password, and so on. The operating system for NUMA-Q systems is called DYNIX/ptx.

Device Drivers

The third and final layer of software in our model is the device driver layer (highlighted in Figure 2.19). Device driver is a term for a set of highly specialized programs, usually written by the manufacturer of computer hardware. These specialized programs reside in main memory or in memory provided right on the adapters they control.

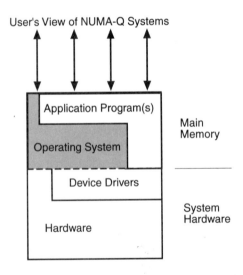

Figure 2.18. The operating system software layer, highlighted in the software model above, provides the environment in which the application programs run.

Unlike application programs or operating systems, other programs only use device drivers. That is, device drivers never interact directly with the users and exist only to help application programs and the operating system perform their tasks. They interact directly with computer hardware elements under the control of the operating system or application program layers. Device drivers also help shield application programs from the hardware specifics of computers, allowing for evolutionary product improvements without sacrificing application program compatibility.

The DYNIX/ptx Operating System

NUMA-Q systems can run either Windows NT or DYNIX/ptx operating systems (or both). Information on Windows NT can be found earlier in this chapter. Here, we examine the DYNIX/ptx operating system.

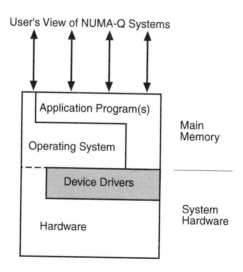

Figure 2.19. The device driver software layer of the software model directly controls the hardware elements of the NUMA-Q application programs and operating systems.

DYNIX/ptx offers an enhanced version of the UNIX operating system that is designed for demanding data center environments. It is a robust and reliable implementation of UNIX designed for SMP (symmetric multiprocessing) and NUMA systems running enterprise-level applications. All processors on NUMA-Q systems are fully symmetric. This means any process can execute on any processor at any time. This symmetric operation is the key to the high-performance and flexible NUMA systems. DYNIX/ptx, with its fully parallelized and threaded kernel, enables linear performance gains within a single operating system image. Thus, as processing resources are added, DYNIX/ptx takes full advantage of every cycle of additional processing power. It is also designed for the Intel 32-bit architecture environment, and provides a low risk path to 64-bit NUMA computing for Intel's IA-64 processors as a part of IBM's Project Monterey. DYNIX/ptx and its layered software products are designed specifically for high-end commercial database management system (DBMS) environments requiring scalability, performance, high availability, and ease of manageability. One way to create manageable, flexible systems is through partitioning of the systems applications.

An important feature has been added to DYNIX/ptx which should further popularize this platform. With the 4.6 release, the operating system supports what is known as the Linux Application Binary Interface (ABI). The Linux ABI allows popular open-source software written to the Linux operating environment to be run unchanged on the NUMA-Q platform. This delivers a truly scalable and data center ready environment for these popular and application programs. With this feature, DYNIX/ptx applications and Linux applications can be run the same machine.

The Application Region Manager

The Application Region Manager is a product integrated into the kernel of the DYNIX/ptx operating system that enables flexibility and control of the computing environment through partitioning. A single instance of DYNIX/ptx running within NUMACenter or NUMA-Q systems can be subdivided into unique, identified application regions. Different applications that represent logical "tiers" in a multitiered architecture can be run in a single managed environment, increasing manageability and cost control, and creating a system that can quickly adjust to changing user demands. Using Application Region Manager, a system administrator can divide processors into regions and assign processes to those regions. Application region management provides the ability to change application regions without system interruption or termination of processes running in the region.

The Application Region Manager also provides for database server consolidation while separating user systems from one another. This makes it easier to manage the workload of a data center and deploy new applications. DYNIX/ptx can be tuned for each application region to optimize the performance of the supported application type so that workloads with varying resource requirements can be run simultaneously. Single-point monitoring and systems administration of the consolidated server enables high availability of both applications and systems. System resources can be reallocated manually or automatically, so they do not remain idle and can be scaled to meet application needs. This reallocation can be done dynamically, without service interruption. Another advantage to this single system environment with multiple partitions is the access to shared management, backup, and storage resources. Performance and availability of business-critical applications are improved while responding quickly to changing application requirements.

Many data centers are moving to a network-centric computing model that minimizes processing requirements at the client workstations. This is accomplished by moving application logic, system management, and operations control to servers. Since the Application Region Manager provides the ability to deploy new applications in a separate region within a single physical machine, ownership costs can be reduced by reducing the data center's need for complex workstations at the same time speeding the deployment process and reducing down-time required for upgrades and application migration.

Shared-Memory Architecture

DYNIX/ptx has a shared-memory architecture that makes the system appear, from both user and system management perspectives, as a single processor system. This type design is important for extremely high levels of performance in SMP and NUMA architectures. As user requirements increase, additional processors and memory can be added to increase performance. DYNIX/ptx can support very large systems with up to 64 gigabytes of physical memory, 64 processors, and tens of terabytes of disk storage. DYNIX/ptx provides support for Intel's Extended Server Memory Architecture (ESMA) through direct use of PAE 36 page table entries. Support for ESMA allows applications to run in memory beyond the four-gigabyte range without any modifications to the applications.

Communications

DYNIX/ptx enables processing of BI transactions concurrently, offering high-performance communications in complex decision support environments. Oracle's Parallel Query Option and Informix Software's Parallel Data Query technology exploit this capability. These products enable NUMA-Q systems running DYNIX/ptx to achieve industry-leading levels of performance using relational database products for decision support. DYNIX/ptx can be implemented in Local Area Network (LAN) and Wide Area Network (WAN) environments. Multiple systems can be connected via TCP/IP, Ethernet, Fast Ethernet, ATM, Token Ring, or FDDI. DYNIX/ptx also supports higher level software to permit functions such as remote login and file transfer. A variety of industry-standard networking products are supported in the DYNIX/ptx operating system including; Novell NetWare, high-performance Network File System (NFS), Net BIOS networks for integration with PC environments, wide area communications including X.25, as well as, IBM's popular protocols.

High Availability and Manageability

The NUMA-Q and DYNIX/ptx operating environment provide excellent application availability and system uptime. Support for multipath I/O provides continuous data availability through multiple, redundant access paths to each device in the system. Multipath I/O also increases performance in a NUMA-Q system by providing local access to all I/O devices from any processor in the system. When used in a multi-node cluster, the multipath I/O interconnect provides uniform, fully redundant, and fully local access to any shared device from any clustered node.

The Volume Management Software (ptx/SVM) provides enhanced disk management and increased system availability over traditional mirroring products by providing disk striping, disk concatenation, and online disk management. These features allow system administrators to optimize disk performance by moving data between disks while the system is running. Disk drives controlled under ptx/SVM can be dynamically resynchronized with one or more mirrored partners, independent of the disk controller, without taking the system down. The ptx/SVM software also enables online replacement of disks and tapes in the NUMA-Q 1000 and NUMA-Q 2000 peripheral bays. Devices can be taken off-line, replaced, and then restored while the system remains up and running. The ptx/SVM disk mirroring capabilities eliminate downtime normally caused by soft and hard errors in the disk subsystem. Support is also provided for redundant boot disks and the ability to mirror the root and swap devices to minimize system downtime.

The Enhanced File System software (ptx/EFS), also improves availability by dramatically reducing file system recovery time. Depending on the size and complexity of the environment, file systems can be recovered in as little as a few seconds in a single system, or as little as a few minutes in large, multi-node configurations. The ptx/EFS software provides online file system resizing and defragmentation, enabling file system changes without downtime. It also includes support for very long file names, symbolic links, 8-bit characters, and access control lists (ACLs). Disk space quotas and file quotas can be used to limit users to specific amounts of disk space and numbers of files.

In a clustered environment, high availability requires sophisticated coordination among nodes and facilities for quick error recovery. The DYNIX/ptx kernel is designed to deliver integrated clusters capabilities. Through the ptx/CLUSTERS software, advanced error recovery and control is provided through features such as a distributed lock manager and a cluster integrity manager.

Installation of the operating system and layered products is easily managed with the ptx/Install program. The ptx/Install program is a menu-driven interface designed to install the DYNIX/ptx software and optional layered products. It also enables online installation by performing an operating system upgrade to an alternate disk partition while the system is online.

DYNIX/ptx supported manageability software for the data center environment reduces the risk of implementing a business-computing infrastructure and helps manage the total cost of ownership. Operating System Management ptx/ADMIN software provides system administration functions like user account management, disk backup, printer and terminal support, inter-system communications, and configuration management. The Systems Management Infrastructure bundled with the DYNIX/ptx operating system is a standards-based infrastructure that enhances the manageability of the NUMA-Q platforms. This infrastructure provides a consistent base for all network, performance, error, and event management. Management solutions for the DYNIX/ptx operating environment are available from a host of leading vendors including Computer Associates' Unicenter TNG, IBM Tivoli's TME 10, and HP's OpenView IT/Operations. DYNIX/ptx provides multiple levels of security that are certifiable at the C2 level. Access Control Lists (ACLs) can be used to protect critical data, and the audit feature can be used to track data access and key events. User-level security features include login checks and encrypted passwords. DYNIX/ptx also conforms to the leading industry operating system standards and provides international support based on the AT&T Multi-National Language Supplement (MNLS).

Finally, it should be noted that DYNIX/ptx includes an enhanced ANSI C compiler, based on the X3.159-1989 standard. This enhanced C compiler incorporates a highly optimizing code generator that produces very efficient object code for high levels of optimization. Existing C code may be ported with little or no modification. Other development languages supported include C, C++, Fortran 90, and COBOL. For commercial development, Relational Data Base Management software from Informix, CA/Ingres, Oracle, Progress, Sybase, and Unify are also supported.

3

pSeries and RS/6000 Computers

This chapter is devoted to the IBM @server pSeries and RS/6000 families of computers. It starts with an overview of the families and then moves in for a closer look at the design features that make the pSeries and RS/6000 systems unique.

A Glance Backwards

To understand the purpose of the pSeries, RS/6000, and the AIX operating system, it is helpful to be familiar with some history. The AIX operating system is IBM's version of the UNIX operating system, which was originally developed by AT&T Bell Labs in 1969. The original UNIX was not intended to be a commercial product, but rather a tool for use internally by computer programmers at AT&T. In fact, at that time AT&T was not in the business of selling computers or operating systems. However, in 1975 AT&T began to license universities to use the UNIX operating system at no charge. This practice caused the UNIX operating system to become widely used in the academic community. Students quickly took advantage of the freedom in the academic world to make their own improvements to the UNIX operating system, often resulting in new commands that, although obvious to the creator, sometimes seemed cryptic to other users. For example, the BIFF command used to pick up electronic mail stored in the computer system was added to the UNIX operating system. Why BIFF? Because the student who made the enhancement had a dog named Biff that was trained to go out and get the newspaper every morning. Although this freedom to make unstructured improvements to the UNIX operating system helped it become more powerful, it also left holes in areas such as data security and reliability.

In 1981, the University of California at Berkeley offered its own version of the UNIX operating system with many enhancements of its own. Berkeley's version of the UNIX operating system, known as Berkeley Software Distribution 4 (BSD 4), became a very popular operating system in its own right—so much so that most of the enhancements contained in the Berkeley version were incorporated by AT&T's later versions of the UNIX operating system.

The RS/6000 Heritage

Meanwhile, IBM was busy working on the "801 project," which was started in 1975. Named after the building in which it was resident, the 801 project was an experiment to develop a minicomputer that bucked the trend toward complex computer programming instructions. Under the leadership of IBM scientist John Cocke, the 801 approach was to simplify the range of instructions used to perform tasks and optimize the computer to execute this limited range of instructions with extreme efficiency. This approach was called RISC (Reduced Instruction Set Computing).

In January 1986, IBM announced the first product to utilize the RISC approach in the IBM RT PC (for RISC technology personal computer) shown in Figure 3.1. At the same time, IBM introduced its own version of the UNIX operating system to run on the RT personal computer, called the Advanced Interactive eXecutive (AIX) operating system. Later, IBM released versions of the AIX operating system for the smaller IBM Personal System/2 computers and the larger S/370 mainframe computers.

In early 1986, IBM hardware and software engineers in Austin, Texas, began the task of designing a new product family. It became

Figure 3.1. IBM RT system. The System Unit can be seen beside the desk, and the associated display and keyboard are on the desktop.

IBM's second-generation RISC technology, combining the RISC philosophy with more-traditional concepts, with the goal of achieving balanced performance. The result of that effort is the RS/6000 family of products and AIX Version 3—both introduced on February 15, 1990. From there, the RS/6000 family of hardware and AIX were enhanced through a continuous stream of product announcements. Then in October of 2000, IBM changed the name of all its server lines and the RS/6000 family became the IBM eServer pSeries family. In the same announcement, two new UNIX systems of RS/6000 heritage were introduced under the new eserver pSeries brand. Although they carry a new name, they are in fact further extensions of and completely compatible with the RS/6000 line. The remainder of this chapter focuses on the new eserver pSeries systems, the most current RS/6000 models, and the latest version of the AIX operating system.

In general, the UNIX marketplace can be divided into two camps. First, there is the "technical and scientific" community. These users are typically crunching numbers to do things like predict the weather or design the latest high-tech aircraft. The primary concerns of these users are floating-point performance and graphics features or performance. Typically they will be looking at the RS/6000 systems that are built around the POWER3 processor, including the parallel SP model. According to IBM, these kinds of users and applications make up about 40 percent of the current RS/6000 users.

The other primary camp within the UNIX marketplace is typically termed "commercial." This camp deals with banking, manufacturing, and retail, to name a few, as well as the fast-growing area of e-business. Their primary concerns are database performance, reliability, and communications with their other, including older heritage, systems. Typically, commercial users look at the deskside and rack Symmetric MultiProcessing (SMP, described later in this chapter) models of the RS/6000 as well as the scalable SP system. This segment of the market is probably 60 percent of the RS/6000 install base.

These definitions of technical and commercial are certainly not exact. Certainly, many banks crunch lots of numbers. Similarly, United States national labs, such as Lawrence Livermore and Sandia, have large databases of information. But this should give us an idea of the general distribution of RS/6000 users and can also give you an idea of where your application and requirements fit into this market.

Many hundreds of thousands of RS/6000s are currently in use. This market is extremely competitive from a performance and price standpoint. If IBM announces a hot new machine, you can be assured that other vendors will react by dropping their prices and six months later announcing their new performance topping system. A different number of factors account for IBM's continued leadership in this market: worldwide service, technological research and innovation, and one-stop shopping.

Meet the eserver pSeries and RS/6000 Family

The IBM eserver pSeries and RS/6000 families are IBM's second generation of computers based on the RISC architecture (described above) developed in the late 1970s. With this concept, a simple set of programming instructions is used to perform all work within the computer system. Because the instructions are simple, they can be executed at very high speed, and they also lend themselves to a more-efficient implementation of the program being executed. The RISC architecture was first introduced in the IBM RT personal computer, later renamed the IBM RT System. The eserver pSeries and RS/6000 families are based on a second-generation RISC architecture, called the Performance Optimized With Enhanced RISC (POWER) architecture, and its PowerPC, POWER3, and RS64 derivatives. The POWER architecture combines the concepts of the original RISC architecture with a sprinkling of more-traditional concepts to create a system with optimum overall system performance. The first RS/6000 systems (see Figure 3.2) shipped beginning in February 1990.

In late 2000, IBM introduced a massive rebranding of it all its server lines. The new brand name that was introduced is the IBM eserver.

Figure 3.2. An IBM RS/6000 rack system in an office setting.

At the same time, two new UNIX systems of RS/6000 heritage were introduced under the name eserver pSeries line. Although they carry a new name, they are in fact further extensions of and completely compatible with the RS/6000 line. These models will be discussed in this chapter along with the existing RS/6000 models. During this name transition period, we will use the term "RS/6000 family" when referring to the combined pSeries and RS/6000 group of computers. Where a distinction is necessary, the specific name will be used.

The pSeries and RS/6000 family uses the AIX (Advanced Interactive eXecutive) operating system. The AIX operating system is IBM's version of the UNIX operating system, originally developed by AT&T Bell Labs. As mentioned earlier, in the AIX operating system, IBM has combined the basic functions of the UNIX operating system with enhancements made by many other companies and academic institutions. IBM has added many enhancements to the AIX operating system and has adhered to the mainstream industry standards developed to make the systems from various vendors more compatible.

Because the AIX operating system conforms to many industry standards, the pSeries and RS/6000 families are considered open systems. This term simply means that the AIX operating system conforms to standards (programming interfaces, communications protocols, and so on) defined by independent standards bodies rather than utilizing an IBM proprietary set of standards not generally adhered to by other computer manufacturers. The advantage of the open-system strategy comes when an independent software development company writes an application program conforming to these industry standards. Because many computer manufacturers offer open-system computers conforming to these industry standards, the software development company can offer its application program on many different brands of open-system computers. The advantages of open systems to computer users are that after selecting the application program that best meets their needs, the users have more flexibility regarding which brand of open-system computer system to buy; after users have purchased an open-system computer, they can choose from the large body of open application programs to meet new needs as they emerge; and users have the flexibility to purchase multiple open-system computers of different brands knowing that they will be able to interoperate over a communications network.

There are difficulties, however, associated with the open-system concept. First, there are multiple organizations simultaneously defining standards for the same open-system environment. This leads to conflicts and incompatibilities. Further, although open- system computer manufacturers conform to industry standards, they also offer proprietary extensions to help differentiate their open-system computers from those of others. The more a software development firm exploits these proprietary extensions, the more it diverges from the spirit of the open-system concept. Even with these difficulties, the open-system approach provides the most widely compatible environment today and shows great promise for the future.

pSeries and RS/6000 Models

Twelve models make up the current pSeries & RS/6000 families. We will divide them into three categories:

- Desktop or Deskside Models: 150, 170

- Deskside-Only Models: 270, F50, F80

- Rack-Mounted Models: B50, p640-B80, H70, H80, M80, S80, p680-S85

Figure 3.3 shows the pSeries and RS/6000 families at a glance. Briefly, let's examine IBM's naming convention of these systems. Notice that some of the systems have numeric designations only. These are systems that are designed to be used as either a workstation or an entry server. Those systems that start with a 1 are uniprocessors, or systems that have a single microprocessor. The systems starting with a 2 are multiprocessors, meaning they can have more than a single microprocessor in one system.

Models that start with a letter are designed primarily to be used as servers. The alphabetic designation loosely corresponds to the size and performance capabilities of that model. For example, the smallest of these systems is the 3.5 inch high B50 rack drawer. The next highest-performing server is the F50, which is a deskside system. Note also, that the letter has at least thus far been used consistently within the same form factor. For example, all H-series systems are rack drawers, whereas all F-series are floor standing. The M80 is higher-performing than the H-series, and the S80 and pSeries-S85 are the largest and fastest of all.

System Model	Processor (s)	SPEC int95	SPEC fp95	Rel. OLTP	Key point of system
150	Power PC 604e (250 or 375 MHz + 1 MB L2)	11.1	8.78	4.0	Low-cost entry point
170	Power 3-II (333, 400, or 450 MHz + 1,4, or 8 MB L2)	15.1 / 19.8 / 25.3 / 29.0	10.1 / 35.6 / 47.9 / 58.4	6.0 / 10.4 / 14.5 / 15.6	Superior floating point, outstanding graphics performance
270	1, 2, 3 or 4 Power3 - II (375 MHz + 4 or 8 MB L2)	24.3 / 24.5 (uni)	48.2 / 53.2 (uni)	80.3 / 92.0 (4w)	Superior floating point SMP
B50	Power PC 604e (375 MHz + 1 MB L2) p640-B80	15.1	10.1	6.0	Low cost, small package, target ISP/ASP
	1, 2, 3 or 4 Power3 - II (375 MHz + 4 or 8 MB)	24.3 / 24.5 (uni)	48.2 / 53.2 (uni)	80.3 / 92.0 (4w)	High performance low cost rack SMP, strong floating point
F50	1, 2, 3 or 4 PowerPC 604e (332 MHz + .25 MB L2)	14.4 (uni)	12.6 (uni)	32.8 (4w)	Entry price commercial SMP
F80	1, 2, 4 or 6 RS64 - III (450/500 MHz + 2 MB uni or 4 MB SMP)	21.0 (uni)	25.4 (uni)	111.9 (6w)	Powerful deskside for commercial users
H70	1, 2, 3 or 4 RS64 - II (340 MHz + 4 MB L2)	16.0 (uni)	21.2 (uni)	57.1 (4w)	Mid-range SMP commercial rack system
H80	1, 2, 4 or 6 RS64 - III (450/500 MHz + 2 MB uni or 4 MB SMP)	21.0 (uni)	25.4 (uni)	111.9 (6w)	Scalable/affordable/powerful mid-range commercial rack system
M80	2, 4, 6 or 8 RS64 - III (500 MHz + 4 MB L2)	24.1 (uni)	29.1 (uni)	222.5 (8w)	Very high performance in rack drawer
S80	6, 12, 18 or 24 RS64 - III (450 MHz + 8 MB L2) p680-S85 6, 12, 18 or 24 RS64 - IV (600 MHz + 16 MB L2)			533.3 (24w) / (24w)	High reliability, high-end enterprise performance 736Industry's highest performing UNIX SMP

Figure 3.3. The IBM @server pSeries and RS/6000 family at a glance.

Let's take a closer look at the pSeries and RS/6000 families. In general, the desktop systems provide from 9.1 to 54.6 GB or more of internal disk storage, over 1 TB of external disk storage, from 128 MB to 2 GB of memory, and five or six expansion slots. This moderate number of expansion slots is usually quite sufficient because all of these systems will include Ethernet LAN and SCSI expansion capabilities on the planar or motherboard without requiring the use of any slots. In addition, like many of today's personal computers, a business audio capability is included in some of IBM's desktop RS/6000's. Standard and maximum configurations will obviously vary from system to system, but this gives you a general idea.

Desktop systems will also operate while on their sides, but the deskside-only systems are strictly floor-standing models. They typically provide more capacity both in internal bays and memory than the desktop systems. The rack systems provide the greatest capacities of memory, disk, slots, and easy expansion. The largest of these can have up to 96 GB of memory, 56 expansion slots, and external disk can be added to dozens of TB. With the rack systems, the system unit is installed into a tall, floor-standing cabinet as shown earlier in Figure 3.2. In fact, the rack has its own model number, the latest being the T00, and is ordered separately. More than one system or peripheral drawer can be placed in a single T00 rack.

pSeries and RS/6000 System Overview

A significant change in the architecture of the RS/6000 systems began back in 1995. At this time IBM began introducing RS/6000s using the industry-standard Peripheral Component Interconnect (PCI) and in some cases the Industry Standard Architecture (ISA) bus structures rather than the proprietary Micro Channel (MCA) bus. These PCI/ISA systems represented a major paradigmshift for the RS/6000 product line. Along with this change, the RS/6000 Division began a move from a line of specialized machines with custom-built components in fairly low volumes to a more generalized line of systems with common off-the-shelf components. There are advantages here for both the user and IBM. IBM can now design new systems and release them to the market faster than the competition. In addition, because of the use of fairly common, high-volume parts, including some used in the

Personal Computer line (e.g., power supplies, cables, disks, memory, etc.) prices to the user continue to drop.

Desktop Systems

Desktop systems are the smallest configurations available and very much resemble the typical personal computer. These systems are often used as engineering workstations and entry performance level servers.

The Model 150 is a PowerPC 604e system with an improved memory controller over its predecessor 140. The processor is available in either 250 MHz or 375 MHz speeds. With a variety of graphics adapters available, this system can perform complex three-dimensional graphics work at a very affordable cost. It is also very well suited for use as a workgroup server. Figure 3.4 shows the Model 150 in a multimedia workstation configuration.

Figure 3.4. RS/6000 Model 43P-150 with P72 monitor and IBM multimedia kit.

The Model 170 is the first 64-bit uniprocessor workstation in the product line. Its POWER3-II microprocessor, employing IBM's innovative new copper design, runs at speeds of either 333 MHz, 400 MHz, or 450 MHz. Its outstanding floating point performance results in an impressive graphics and technical workload system at a very attractive price. As the least expensive 64-bit system available, it is also a great choice for software development and testing.

The larger enclosures of the deskside models we will now discuss are designed to sit on the floor and allow these models to accommodate more main memory, more disk storage, and more I/O adapters. Do not discount using these systems in single-user graphics environment, in which the 150 and 170 are more typically used. Armed with a graphics adapter and monitor, the 200-series deskside systems can make excellent workstations.

Deskside Systems

The RS/6000 Model 270 (Figure 3.5) is a second generation multiprocessing workstation or server. As such, it sports up to 4 POWER3-II microprocessors running at 375 MHz. Equipped with a three-dimensional graphics adapter card, the 270 delivers industry-leading three-dimensional graphics performance. It is also a very cost-effective midrange server for both technical and commercial workloads with leading price/performance in applications such as Web-serving.

The RS/6000 Model F50 is a deskside, PCI-based, SMP system that supports one to four 604e microprocessors at 332 MHz as well as 256 KB of L2 cache for each processor. The F50 was the first PCI system capable of true enterprise workloads. Because of its price/performance and its ability to hold up to 336 GB of internal disk, this system has been one of the most popular in the RS/6000 product line. Although it is getting on in years, its price performance as an OnLine Transaction Processing (OLTP) system, a Web server, and a Lotus Notes server is still very competitive.

The Model F80 is among the newest of the commercial servers. This floor-standing system is the heir to the position long held by the F50 as the best cost performance on the floor. With one, two, or four RS64-III copper-based processors running at 450 MHz, or six processors running at 500 MHz, the F80 is an excellent choice for small

Figure 3.5. RS/6000 Model 43P-260 dual-processor workstation.

and medium-sized businesses to run their e-business, enterprise resource planning (ERP), Web hosting, and datamart applications.

Rack-Mounted Systems

Two rack systems are based on the aforementioned deskside systems. The new pSeries 640 Model B80 (Figure 3.6) is essentially a rack form factor for the Model 270. It is designed for ease of manageability with front access and alert lights. The Model H80 is a rack form of the F80 system. The H80, shown in Figure 3.7, delivers the same performance but uses an innovative modular design in which capacity and PCI I/O slots (up to 28) can be added as needed.

The Model H70 has no deskside equivalent and uses 1 to 4 RS64-II processors running at 340 MHz. This system is a 64-bit follow-on and

Figure 3.6.   The IBM @server pSeries 640 Model B80 is a compact rack drawer with up to four processors.

natural replacement for the discontinued 32-bit Model H50. It performs commercial workloads about 60 to 70 percent faster than the H50.

Another of the newer models, the M80, pushes the upper limit of what has been considered midrange performance. This 2-, 4-, 6-, or 8-way SMP system also uses the 500 MHz copper RS64-III microprocessor. With an internal switch architecture previously used only on the high-end S-series, the M80 delivers excellent performance of all commercial workloads. It can be configured with up to 32 MB of memory and uses the same modular expansion scheme as the H80, but allowing for as many as 56 PCI slots in a single system.

The Model S80 is a 24-way rack-based system that introduced the PowerPC RS64-III copper microprocessor with 8 MB of L2 cache per processor. The S80 is a 64-bit system supported, like all the other systems, by IBM's 64-bit AIX Version 4.3. This system is designed to give superior performance and price performance in commercial applications such as OLTP. As we will see in the detailed discussion of

Figure 3.7. A front view of the rack-mounted RS/6000 Model H80 with a single RIO drawer.

this model, it is a large system built with reliability and high-availability features standard.

The IBM eserver pSeries 680 Model S85 is the current flagship of the IBM line. A natural successor to the position held by the S80, the p680 has up to twenty-four 600 MHz RS64-IV copper and Silicon-on-Insulator (SOI) processors, in increments of 6, and as much as 96 GB of main memory. This processor and memory upgrade has yielded a system roughly 40 percent more powerful than the S80, and is currently on the top of the heap in many commercial benchmarks. As this book was being published, the p680, shown in Figure 3.8, delivers performance that surpasses all other UNIX SMP systems in a number of benchmarks including TPC-C (a measure of online transaction processing), Web serving, and Lotus Notes. It is appropriate for the largest of all workloads, and with the use of the AIX workload management feature is a great platform for consolidating multiple workloads.

Figure 3.8. The industry-leading commercial SMP system is the IBM @server pSeries 680 Model S85 with up to 24 copper and Silicon-on-Insulator processors.

The pSeries and RS/6000 families include systems designed to meet the needs of either technical users (engineers, scientists, economists, and so on) or general-purpose commercial users (executives, accountants, clerks, secretaries, and so on). The various models along with numerous options and peripherals offer many different levels of performance, capacity, and function.

POWERparallel SP

The IBM Scalable POWERparallel System 9076 SP1 was the first system to employ multiple RS/6000 main processors in a single system. The family of IBM's parallel processors continued to be enhanced with the SP2. In 1996 the systems' numeric designator was dropped, they were moved into the mainline of the RS/6000 family, and they are now called RS/6000 SP (Figure 3.9).

Systems that employ multiple main processors working in parallel can achieve extremely high levels of performance and are called highly parallel or massively parallel systems (depending on the number of main processors used in the system). A common industry term is Massively

Figure 3.9. The IBM Scalable POWERparallel SP system.

Parallel Processing (MPP). This may sound very much like the SMP systems that we discussed earlier, but the SP is quite different. Because the processors within the SP do not share a single operating system, disk, memory, or adapters, the SP is called a "shared nothing" environment. This allows hundreds of processors to be combined in a SP rather than only a few in the SMP. Later in this chapter we will examine both the SMP and parallel-processing environments in more detail.

From a hardware perspective, the SP consists of a frame, which then contains the various processing nodes. Nodes can be of various types, some based largely on an existing standalone RS/6000 model, but repackaged to fit the SP. These nodes are referred to as thin, wide, high, and external. At one time nodes could be uniprocessors, but today all nodes are SMPs. These nodes can also be of different processor speeds within the same SP frame. Nodes available today are based on the RS/6000 Model 270 (SMP thin or wide), a unique 16-way node (high), and (externally) S80/p680. See Figure 3.10 for a summary of the various nodes.

The frame provides the interconnection among all of the nodes. This interconnection can be either just Ethernet LAN or an additional SP Switch (SPS). The SP Switch provides a high-speed, low-latency, point-to-point connection for all nodes in the frame, making distributed applications more efficient. Like the standalone RS/6000 systems, the SP also supports node interconnection by any of the standard LAN adapters such as token-ring, FDDI, ATM, and so on. An SP system can have as few as 1 or as many as 512 nodes contained in from 1 to over 30 frames.

Frames come in two different sizes (see Figure 3.11)—short (49 inches with four drawers) or tall (79 inches with eight drawers). A drawer contains the space and appropriate mounting hardware and connections for the various nodes. Thin nodes, as the name suggests, are small and take up only half of a drawer. However, thin nodes typically are purchased in pairs, thus consuming an entire drawer of space. Wide nodes, because of their additional slots and bays, take up a full drawer. IBM's largest type of internal node, first announced in July 1996, is the high node. The high node, again as its name implies, takes up twice as much space as wide nodes, thus consuming two drawers within a SP frame. Currently, IBM supports a maximum of 64 high nodes in a single SP system. External nodes, as their name indicates, are nodes that are logically part of the SP system but are not enclosed in the SP frame. The first examples of these are the Sxx nodes. The RS/6000 Models S70, S80, and p680 can be attached as nodes to the SP. (Observing the size of these systems, one can easily conclude that if this high-end SMP system were to be part of the SP, it would have to participate from outside the frame.) They can also attach to the SP Switch through a PCI switch adapter (feature code 8396). Attachment of these large systems to the SP introduces the possibility of several different applications servers (internal SP nodes) accessing a single, very large, SMP database system (external SP node), while allowing central management.

An additional piece of hardware called the Control Workstation (CWS) is required to complete the SP. This is a standalone RS/6000 (frequently a Model 150 with graphics) that manages all the nodes

Mode Type

Features	375 MHz Power3 SMP Thin	375 MHz Power3 SMP Wide	375 MHz Power3 SMP High	Model S80 (External)	pSeries 680 Model S85 (External)
CPU Power3 - II RS64-III RS64-IV	2 or 4 @ 375 MHz —	2 or 4 @ 375 MHz —	4,8,12,16 @ 375 MHz —	— 6,12,18,24 @450 MHz or 600 MHz	— 6,12,18,24 @600 MHz
Slots PCI 32-bit PCI 64-bit	2 —	2 8	1 up to 52	33 20	33 20
Disk/Media Bays	2	4	2 up to 26	48/8	48/8
Memory (MB) Standard Maximum Level 2 (per CPU)	256 16 GB 8	256 16 GB 8	1024 64 GB 8	2048 96 GB 8or 16	4096 96 GB 16
Disk (GB) Standard Internal Maximum	0 36.4	0 109.2	0 946.4	9.1 873.6	9.1 873.6
Performance SPECint_ base_rate 95 SPECfp_ base_rate 95 Relative OLTP	407/812 804/1359 44/67.7	407/812 804/4359 44/80	786/1569/ 2345/3121 1670/3290/ 4832/6202 81.7/160.3/ 242.3/319.3	139/265/ 369.1/452.7	213.3/405/ 548.6/716.6

Figure 3.10. Comparison matrix for SP nodes.

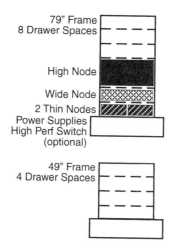

79" Frame
8 Drawer Spaces

High Node

Wide Node
2 Thin Nodes
Power Supplies
High Perf Switch
(optional)

49" Frame
4 Drawer Spaces

Figure 3.11.   The Powerparallel SP frames are either 79" or 49" tall.

within the SP. The CWS is the repository for the Single System Image (SSI). The SSI gives a single interface to the users and systems administrators of the SP. This is typically the most daunting challenge to putting tens or hundreds of processors together on a single task—making it look like just one system when it is in fact hundreds of systems. The SSI provides a single copy of the AIX operating system, which is then proliferated to each node.

The SP was originally very popular for large-scale numeric computing environments such as research centers and universities. This was an area typically dominated by supercomputers like Cray, Convex, or IBM mainframes. With the appearance of parallel databases like Oracle Versions 7 and 8 and IBM's DB/2 Universal Database (UDB), the SP has also been popular in commercial database processing as well. A third application area, called LAN consolidation, has emerged for the SP. Instead of having RS/6000 servers geographically distributed throughout an enterprise to locations where systems administrators might not be on-site, some users find that using the SP can be a very cost-effective alternative. By using a common pool of administrative personnel, backup devices, printers, and storage, the SP provides the benefits of high-performance RISC workstations and servers with centralized, cost-effective systems administration. Figure 3.12 illustrates how one SP user may decide to distribute workload to various nodes. Today, use of the SP in the commercial market has far outpaced use in this technical market, although SP systems in this market generally do contain larger numbers of nodes.

pSeries and RS/6000 Hardware Architecture

The internal organization of the hardware elements making up the pSeries or RS/6000 system is known as its hardware architecture. The architecture of pSeries and RS/6000 computers contributes a great deal to the performance offered by these systems. The pSeries and RS/6000 architecture is an enhanced version of the earlier RISC architecture. As explained earlier, with RISC the instruction set or total number of programming instructions that can be executed within the computer is reduced compared with more-traditional CISC (Complex Instruction Set Computing). Because the instructions in RISC systems are very simple, they can be executed using high-speed computer hardware within the computer system in a very short period of time (for example, one clock cycle). Further, the simple instruction

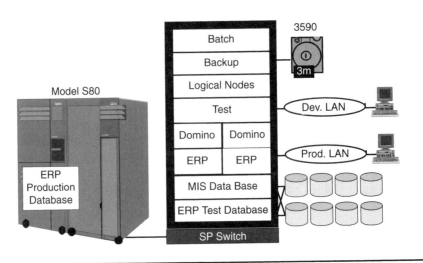

Figure 3.12. One possible way of distributing workload within an SP system.

set of a RISC computer typically can be carefully employed to perform even complex functions in a more-efficient manner.

This original RISC architecture was first used in the earlier IBM RT system, which had limited success. The pSeries and RS/6000 families employs IBM's second-generation RISC architecture, called the POWER (Performance Optimized With Enhanced RISC) architecture. As previously discussed, this architecture utilizes a blend of the original RISC architecture and some traditional CISC concepts with an emphasis on doing multiple operations at the same time. The new PowerPC architecture, developed jointly by IBM, Apple, and Motorola, is a highly compatible derivative of the POWER architecture. Currently, the PowerPC architecture (discussed later in this chapter) is implemented on all of the pSeries and RS/6000 models. Earlier systems in the RS/6000 family were based on the POWER architecture and implemented either with the POWER2 multichip main processor design or the more powerful POWER2 single-chip design, called the POWER2 Super Chip (P2SC).

To understand the POWER architecture, it is necessary to look at two key pieces of pSeries and RS/6000 systems—the main processor and the main memory system. The main processor and the main memory system, along with other circuits, make up the Central Processing Unit (CPU) circuit board found inside the pSeries and RS/6000 chassis.

The smallest piece of information the main processor and main memory can use is called a bit. These bits are grouped into bytes (8 bits), half-word (16 bits), words (32 bits), and double words (64 bits) to form the computer's representation of numbers, letters of the alphabet, instructions in a program, and so on. With this basic knowledge, we can examine the pSeries and RS/6000 system's main processor and main memory.

The Main Processor

The main processor is the heart of a computer system because it is the control center for information flow inside the computer. It is the main processor that does the data manipulation, or "thinking," necessary to perform tasks for the user. The speed of the circuits making up the main processor, along with the architecture of the main processor, determines the overall processing speeds achievable by the computer system.

Several different (though compatible) main processor designs have been used in the RS/6000 product line, including:

- The original implementation of the POWER architecture, which is no longer used in today's RS/6000 models

- A RISC Single Chip (RSC) implementation of the POWER architecture built within a single chip

- PowerPC 601, 603, 604, and 604e, and RS64, RS64-II, RS64-III, and RS64-IV microprocessors, which provide significant performance at lower costs

- A POWER2 multichip implementation of the POWER architecture that provides high-speed performance for numeric- and graphics-intensive applications

- A POWER2 single-chip implementation that has even higher performance than the multichip design in the same applications

- The POWER3 single-chip design, which falls into the PowerPC architecture but adds the strength of POWER2 characteristics for excellent floating-point and graphics workloads.

We can get a feel for the strengths of the POWER architecture by taking a quick look at the original implementation. There are five basic elements in the original RS/6000 main processor architecture, each made up of thousands of circuits packaged in several specially designed chips:

1. Instruction cache/branch

2. Fixed-point processor

3. Floating-point processor

4. Data cache

5. I/O unit

Figure 3.13 is a block diagram showing how these elements are organized to make up the pSeries and RS/6000 hardware architecture. To see how this architecture can do multiple operations at the same time, we can trace the flow of information through the system. It all starts when the user executes a command to start a program,

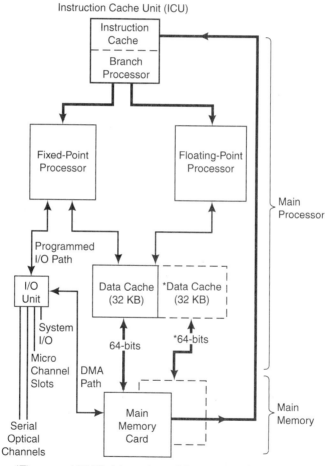

*The second 32 KB data cache and the second 64-bit data path are only provided on the larger RS/6000 Models.

Figure 3.13. RS/6000 POWER architecture original multichip implementation.

which causes the instructions of that program to be retrieved from disk storage and loaded into main memory (shown at the bottom of the diagram). After the program is loaded into main memory, the main processor requests the very first instruction (4 bytes) in the program. In compliance with the request, the first instruction, along with the next several instructions (a total of 64 sequential bytes), is retrieved from the main memory and is loaded into the Instruction Cache Unit (ICU). The instruction cache is a group of very high-speed memory circuits contained in the ICU chip. It is used as a temporary holding area (8 KB in size) for programming instructions that are likely to be next in line to be executed.

When the main processor requests the next instruction, it first looks in the ICU. Most of the time, the next instruction needed will already have been loaded into the ICU, eliminating the delay associated with getting the instruction from slower main memory. This is called a cache hit. Because the instruction cache can respond much more quickly than the system's main memory, system performance is dramatically improved with every cache hit. If the needed instruction is not already loaded into the ICU (called a cache miss), another 64 bytes starting with the needed instruction are automatically loaded from the main memory into the ICU. In the case of a cache miss, loading the ICU takes longer than simply getting the needed instruction from main memory (that is, a cache miss results in a penalty to system performance), so it is a game of statistics. Because most computer programs will experience many more cache hits than misses during normal operation, the cache technique usually increases overall system performance significantly.

So far, then, we have gotten the first few programming instructions loaded into the 8 KB of instruction cache memory located in the ICU. Next, the branch processor component of the ICU examines each programming instruction in turn and independently executes any condition register or branch instructions. Condition register instructions manipulate the contents of working storage locations (a condition register) within the main processor that stores information about the results of calculations performed earlier in the program. Branch instructions are a commonly used type of programming instruction that directs the flow of the program, usually taking different paths depending on the contents of the condition register. Branch instructions that are executed completely within the ICU (while other operations are happening in the other processor elements) are said to occur in zero system clock cycles. These branches are therefore said to be zero cycle branches.

While the branch processor intercepts and executes branch and condition register instructions, the remaining instructions are simultaneously fed to and executed by the fixed-point and floating-point processors. The fixed-point processor performs mathematical and logical operations with things that don't have decimal points, such as whole numbers (for example, the integers 1, 5, and 6) and numeric representations of text (such as ASCII codes). These fixed-point instructions are common in almost any computing environment. The floating-point processor performs mathematical and logical operations (IEEE 754-1985) with things that have a decimal point (that is, real numbers such as 53.254376, 4.6, and 3.1313). These floating-point instructions are common in engineering/scientific applications and others requiring sophisticated computer graphics.

For anyone who isn't counting, that makes four independent operations going on inside the main processor at the same time:

1. A branch instruction

2. A condition register instruction

3. A fixed-point instruction

4. A floating-point instruction

In fact, if the floating-point instruction happens to be the multiply–add (A x B + C) or the multiply–subtract (A x B – C) instruction, these can be counted as two floating-point operations, making a total of five operations being performed at once. This architecture is therefore said to be a superscalar implementation.

The instruction cache and processing units in the main processor allow an system to execute a great many programming instructions in a very small amount of time. However, it is not enough to make a main processor architecture that offers high performance. You must also be able to efficiently move the data on which the programming instructions are to operate between the main processor and main memory. This is where the data cache unit comes in. The data cache unit operates much like the instruction cache unit, only the data cache unit provides a temporary holding area for data needed during program execution rather than programming instructions. When a program instruction requires data on which to operate, the data cache unit is first checked to see if the needed data has already been loaded. If the data cache unit contains the needed data (a cache hit), it can very quickly provide the needed information and dramatically boost system performance. If the data cache unit does not have the requested data, a cache miss occurs, which negatively impacts system performance. In the event of a cache miss, the needed data plus the next few words of data are automatically loaded from the slower main memory to the data cache unit.

In this way, the data cache unit continuously accumulates the data most likely to be needed during upcoming calculations, increasing the likelihood of cache hits. As with the ICU, the more cache hits, the better the system performance. Statistically speaking, the larger the data cache, the higher the percentage of cache hits, and thus the higher the overall system performance.

The base models of the RS/6000 family have a data cache 32 KB in size, whereas the larger models have a 64 KB data cache, accounting in part for their higher performance. Still other processors, such as the PowerPC 601, have a combined 32-KB data and instruction cache. Those models with the 64-KB data cache are also designed to move twice as much information between main memory and the data cache. That is, the models with the 64-KB data cache provide a more-efficient path (for example, a 128-bit-wide data path versus a 64-bit-wide data path on models with the 32-KB data cache) between main memory and the data cache, which also serves to boost system performance. All pSeries and RS/6000 models use a scheme called set associativity to reduce the number of instruction and cache misses by allowing for more-efficient sharing of the data cache among multiple programs running simultaneously.

Finally, the Input/Output Unit (I/O Unit) element of the main processor manages data transfers between all input/output devices and the rest of the computer system. These include things such as the disks, communications adapters installed in the micro channel slots, and any devices attached to serial optical channels. Often, the information will flow directly between the I/O device and main memory. This is called Direct Memory Access (DMA). Other times, the program may directly control the information between the main processor and the I/O device. This is called programmed I/O.

The activities of the five processor elements are coordinated by an electronic signal called the system clock. The system clock is the heartbeat of the computer system. It takes the main processor through each step in the execution of a program. It is the time reference of the main processor and sets the pace for all main processor activity. The speed at which the system clock runs is called the system clock rate and is measured in millions of clock steps per second, or megahertz (MHz). For example, the RS/6000 Model 150 runs at 375 MHz and the Model S80 runs at 450 MHz. The system clock rate of the microprocessor is very important to the performance of a computer system. However, there are many other things inside a computer (such as main processor architecture/implementation, instruction sets, main memory system speeds, disk speeds, I/O bus speeds, and so on) that together define the overall performance of a computer system. Therefore, comparing individual specifications (for example, the system clock rate) of computer systems can be very misleading.

Main Memory

The main memory is also a very important part of a computer. Main memory is the set of electronic chips that provide a "workspace" for the main processor. That is, it holds the information (program instructions and data) being used by the main processor. As mentioned earlier, this main memory is called Random Access Memory (RAM) because it can store and retrieve information independently of the sequential order in which it was originally stored.

The smallest RS/6000 systems come standard with 128 MB (about 128 million bytes) of main memory. The largest systems can have up to 96 GB (about 96 billion bytes) of main memory. When you have this much main memory in a system, schemes to detect and correct memory defects become necessary to protect the integrity of the information stored in the computer system. The pSeries and RS/6000 uses several techniques to protect the integrity of its main memory. The Error Checking and Correction (ECC) technique used by members of the pSeries and RS/6000 family can detect single- and double-bit errors and can correct single-bit errors. This is done by appending seven additional bits (called ECC bits) onto every word (32 bits) in main memory. The seven ECC bits are automatically generated by the ECC circuitry based on the value of the associated word and are then stored in main memory alongside that word. New ECC bits are calculated and stored every time a word is written to main memory. Later, when that word is read back from main memory, the value stored in the corresponding ECC bits is checked to make sure that the word didn't somehow get corrupted through some type of main memory failure. The most common type of failure is to have a single bit in the word accidentally get changed to the wrong value. In this case, the ECC circuitry can use the value stored in the ECC bits to actually correct the error on the fly and allow normal operations to continue undisturbed. On rare occasions, a main memory failure will cause two bits in a single word to be changed. In this case, the ECC circuitry can only detect and report the error. In addition to monitoring all read/write activity in main memory, the ECC circuitry periodically scans all of main memory to ensure the integrity of the information. This is called memory "scrubbing." The pSeries and RS/6000 main memory employs some other techniques to ensure the integrity of the system: bit scattering, memory bus parity, and bit steering.

Bit scattering means that memory chips used to make up the main memory system are organized in a way that minimizes the impact of a single chip failure. Memory bus parity refers to an extra bit appended to the parallel group of wires (called a bus) used to transfer information to and from main memory. This extra bit, called a parity bit, is used to detect any errors that may occur as the information is transferred along the memory bus. In fact, parity bits are used on chip-to-chip data buses and throughout most internal chip data paths. Finally, "bit steering" is a concept in which extra memory bits designed into the main memory system can be used to replace failing bits, in many cases without disrupting normal operation. The extra bit is "steered" onto the memory bus in place of the failing bit. All of these things help protect the integrity of the information in the computer system and allow it to recover from errors without disturbing users.

In any computer system, a great deal of information is moving in and out of main memory. For this reason, the design of the main memory can significantly affect overall system performance. There are two major reasons that so much time is spent moving information in and out of the main memory. First, the programming instructions of the active program(s) reside in the main memory. Therefore, every instruction in the program must at some point be retrieved from the main memory. Second, the main memory holds and accepts data used in the program(s) being executed. If the overall information flow to and from main memory (assisted by the instruction cache unit and the data cache unit) cannot keep pace with the main processor, the main processor will be delayed and system performance will suffer. For this reason, the main memory must be designed to keep up with the speeds achievable by the main processor.

The design of the pSeries & RS/6000 main processor and its main memory are balanced through the use of separate data and instruction caches and the wide path between main memory and the caches, as discussed earlier. To further balance the system, the path or bus between the caches and main memory (which can operate at up to thousands of MB per second) is independent from the micro channel or PCI bus used for input/output activity such as disk information transfers. This prevents interference between main memory activity and input/output activity, which can decrease the overall performance of the system.

Finally, the pSeries and RS/6000 main memory design uses a technique called interleaving. This is a way of subdividing the memory chips to allow an overlap of multiple transfers to and from main memory; that is, two words of data (64 bits) can be read from a memory card in a single system clock cycle (two-way interleaving). The wider data path of the more-powerful pSeries & RS/6000 models allows the two memory cards to each provide two words per cycle, for a total of four words (128 bits) per cycle (four-way interleaving). Interleaving increases the effective transfer rate between main memory and the caches, ultimately feeding the main processor with the necessary programming instructions and data.

Memory Management

The way in which a computer system utilizes available main memory and disk storage is called the computer's memory management scheme and is basic to the capabilities of the computer. Understanding memory management is critical to understanding one of the features of pSeries and RS/6000 computers. Figure 3.14 is a conceptual view of memory in pSeries and RS/6000 systems. The main memory is contained inside the computer's system unit. The disk storage may be inside the system unit or in a separate box cabled to the system unit.

When the computer system is first turned on, information vital to an orderly start-up and smooth operation is automatically copied from disk storage to the main memory. Once normal system operation is

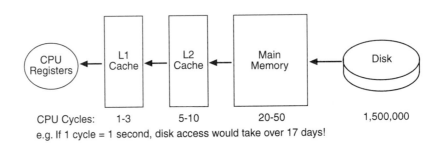

CPU Cycles: 1-3   5-10   20-50   1,500,000
e.g. If 1 cycle = 1 second, disk access would take over 17 days!

Figure 3.14. Conceptual view of the RS/6000 main memory and disk storage illustrating the value and speed of large cache and memory over disk storage.

established, users can begin to do their work. During the course of this work, the user will start various computer programs. As the user starts each program, it is copied from disk storage to main memory and then executed. Based on the work the user is doing, the computer programs manipulate various sets of data that are also loaded from the disk storage to main memory as needed. The main memory in a computer can quickly become filled up with programs and data as the system is called upon to do more and more work. In earlier days of computing, the main memory size limited the amount of work a computer could manage at any one time. This limitation capped the size of programs, the number of programs that could be run concurrently, the number of users who could share the system, and so on.

In today's environment, a technique called virtual memory alleviates the need to squeeze all active programs and data into main memory. In computers that support virtual memory, the computer basically "fakes out" the computer programs, making the computer system appear to have much more main memory than it actually has. The largest of today's pSeries and RS/6000 systems can have 96 GB of main memory. The virtual memory supported by all pSeries and RS/6000 systems is a whopping 4 TB (terabytes) in size (2 raised to the power 52, or over 4,500 trillion bytes). The pSeries and RS/6000 system's 4 TB of addressing capability is enough to keep track of the information contained on over 2 trillion pages of single-spaced computer output. That is a stack of paper over 200,000 miles high—almost reaching the moon.

Virtual memory therefore allows more programs, data, and users to be simultaneously active on the system than could be supported in real main memory without virtual memory. That is, it allows you to make the most out of whatever size main memory you actually have.

Here is how virtual memory works: Say a user tells the computer to start a word processing program. The computer first attempts to load the needed portion of the word processing program into main memory. If no space is left in main memory, some space will be made available by overwriting an inactive portion of some program or by swapping some inactive data to a temporary space in disk storage. The needed portion of the word processing program can then be loaded into the available space and the user can begin typing. If the program that was overwritten or the data that was swapped out is needed again, it will be reloaded from disk storage to some other available main memory area. So a virtual memory computer system is constantly swapping programs and information between main memory and disk storage. Virtual memory allows the maximum size program or combination of all programs and data to be limited only by the combined amount of main memory and disk storage rather than by the amount of main memory size alone. The advantage of having this virtual memory built into the pSeries and RS/6000 hardware and AIX operating system is that neither the programmers nor the users of any pSeries and RS/6000 system need be concerned with main memory size. To them, the system seems to have as much main memory as they need, and they are never made aware that information is constantly being swapped from main memory to disk storage and back again. The computer hardware and AIX operating system efficiently manage this swapping (also called paging) automatically.

Virtual memory is a powerful system feature, but it comes at a price. The paging between disk storage and main memory is processing overhead that can reduce the overall system performance. A little paging will not appreciably hurt performance, but the more paging, the more system performance will be reduced. When the paging performed by a virtual memory system gets excessive, the system is said to be "thrashing," or spending too much time paging information between disk storage and main memory. Thrashing can be reduced by increasing the amount of main memory in the system through the installation of memory-expansion options described in Chapter 2. Increasing the size of the main memory system will provide more room for programs and data, reducing the amount of virtual memory paging.

The virtual memory concept is implemented in most of today's computer systems to some degree. pSeries and RS/6000 systems implement their virtual memory scheme through a concept called single-level storage. This term means that in pSeries and RS/6000 systems, no distinction is made between disk storage and main memory. All storage appears to be one homogeneous sea of main memory that is accessed in exactly the same way. This consistency provides for a simple and efficient virtual memory implementation that is the same for programs, data, temporary holding areas, and so on. Other virtual memory implementations must create and manage separate address spaces, and they often treat programs differently than they do data, for example. The simplicity of the single-level storage design results in a consistent and more-complete virtual memory system than that of most other implementations.

Symmetric Multiprocessing

IBM's Symmetric MultiProcessor (SMP) RS/6000 systems use a design that combines the PowerPC microprocessor, AIX operating systems, and IBM's large systems development experience. The basic design of any SMP system (Figure 3.15) involves multiple processors (CPUs) accessing a common, shared set of resources (for example, memory, fixed disk, communication adapters, and operating system). The processors communicate with each other and main memory via the internal bus or parallel data switch.

Each processor in the system will be performing separate jobs or running different programs at any one point in time (for example, database access, terminal interaction, or network communication). Figure 3.15 gives you a look inside a symmetric multiprocessing system at a single point in time with several applications running on the system. It is important to say "single point in time" because in the next few ticks of the system clock, these applications, in a true multitasking environment, have an equal chance to be rescheduled on the same or other CPUs in the complex. The applications will also be swapped out when they have exhausted their time-slice to let other programs run.

A single application program can be designed and tuned to an SMP architecture such that it will subdivide and run on multiple pro-

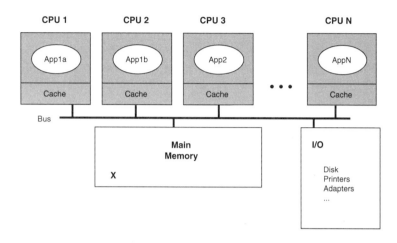

Figure 3.15. Basic design of typical N-way symmetric multiprocessor.

cessors in the SMP system at the same time (App1a and App1b in Figure 3.15). However, this takes special design and coding on the part of the programmers, so today, more often than not, programs will be left to run much as they do on a uniprocessor (App2 and AppN). Not that this is bad (indeed, SMP systems allow many of these independent applications to run at the same time, each scheduled to a single CPU), but in this example, App1 should be able to achieve greater overall throughput than if it had been limited to a single processor. Often this throughput is well worth the coding effort for database developers. If you are purchasing a database, however, the development and tuning work has already been done for you. Often database users will be able to bring forward all of their investment in queries, screens, reports, and so on. They may require only a minor modification or recompilation when moving from the uniprocessor version of the database to the SMP version.

pSeries and RS/6000 Software

The previous sections examined the various models of the pSeries and RS/6000 family. This section begins our look at how you put that hardware to work—namely, the all-important software. Software is a general term for the many programs that execute in computers. It is software that harnesses the pSeries and RS/6000 system's computational power and allows you to perform many diverse and useful tasks.

Types of Software—A Conceptual Model

There are different categories of software, diverse in function and purpose. The basic categories of "real software" used in pSeries and RS/6000 systems can be understood through the model shown in Figure 3.16. There are three basic categories, or software layers, used in pSeries and RS/6000 systems: the application program layer, the operating system layer, and the device driver layer. Each software layer performs a completely different job, but all three work closely together to perform useful work for the user. Although some special-purpose programs do not fit neatly into any of these three categories, the majority of software does. Below is examination of each of the three layers in our software model.

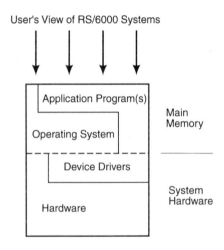

Figure 3.16. The three layers of the RS/6000 system's basic software structure, shown in the conceptual software model above, work together to perform useful work for the user.

Application Programs

The top software layer in the software model is the application program layer (highlighted in Figure 3.17). The programs in this layer "apply" a computer system to a specific task (computer-aided design, transaction processing, data mining, etc.) and thus are called "application" programs. They actually perform the task for which the user purchased the computer while the other two layers play important support roles. A single computer system might run one application program at a time, or it might run many application programs simultaneously.

The arrows in the figure indicate how users conceptually "see" the computer system. The user usually interacts with the application program layer and (less frequently) the operating system layer. By working closely with the other software layers, the application program processes the various keystrokes made by the user and responds by displaying information on the computer's display or some other output device. As we will see later, many application programs written for other computers that run another variant of the UNIX oper-

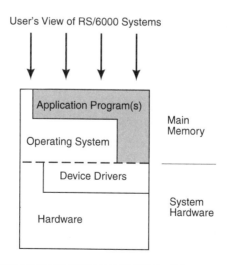

Figure 3.17. The application program software layer, highlighted in the software model above, is the application program that defines the particular task the company is performing for the user.

ating system (i.e., open systems) can be migrated to pSeries and RS/6000 systems by the software developer.

Operating Systems

The next layer in our software model is the operating system (highlighted in Figure 3.18). The operating system must manage the hardware resources of the computer system and perform tasks under the control of application program(s) and keyboard/mouse commands issued by the user. The application program can rely on the operating system to perform many of the detailed housekeeping tasks associated with the internal workings of the computer. Thus, the operating system is said to provide the environment in which application programs execute. The operating system layer also accepts commands directly from the user; for instance, it can copy files, change a user's password, and so on.

The operating systems used on pSeries and RS/6000 systems provide an environment that can run one application program at a time or many application programs simultaneously. There are also many extensions to the AIX operating system, such as the graphics program

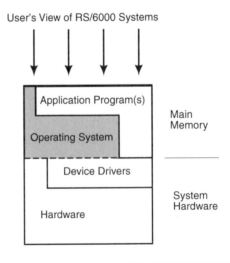

Figure 3.18. The operating system software layer, highlighted in the software model above, provides the environment in which the application programs run.

OpenGL, that allow the user to customize the operating system environment. Because of the modular nature of AIX, these extensions plug right into and essentially become a part of the operating system.

Device Drivers

The third and final layer of software in our software model is the device driver layer (highlighted in Figure 3.19). Device driver is a term for a set of highly specialized programs, usually written by the manufacturer of computer hardware. These specialized programs reside in the pSeries and RS/6000 main memory or in memory provided right on the adapters they control.

Unlike application programs or operating systems, other programs only use device drivers. That is, device drivers never interact directly with the users and exist only to help application programs and the operating system perform their tasks. They interact directly with computer hardware elements under the control of the operating system or application program layers. Device drivers also help shield application programs from the hardware specifics of computers, allowing for evolutionary product improvements without sacrificing application program compatibility.

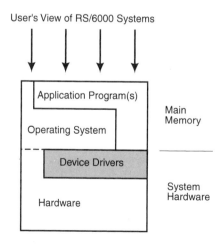

Figure 3.19. The device driver software layer of the software model directly controls the hardware elements of the RS/6000 systems and shields application programs and operating systems from hardware details.

Software Compatibility—Why It Is Important

Computer systems that run the UNIX operating system have been in existence for many years. As a result, a wide variety of application programs have been developed for UNIX. The flexibility afforded by virtue of this large and diverse software base allowed computers running the UNIX operating system to fill many different needs. Of course, this plethora of available application programs did not exist when the original UNIX operating system was first announced. It took the independent efforts of a great many people over many years' time to develop the large number of application programs (called an application program software base) that exist today. In order to capitalize on that software base, application software compatibility was a primary objective in the design of the AIX operating systems. That is, most application programs written for UNIX operating systems can easily be migrated to the pSeries and RS/6000 and AIX operating system by the software developer.

It is important to understand that of the three software layers in our software model, compatibility with programs in the application programs layer is most important. Why? First of all, application programs typically represent the lion's share of a user's software investment. Further, being forced to abandon an application program due to incompatibilities may also make users throw away whatever data and training or experience they have accumulated with the application program—both of which can be substantial. Some users have developed custom application programs at considerable cost in development time and money. Incompatibility at the application program level would render these programs virtually useless. Finally, and perhaps most important, application layer compatibility allows pSeries and RS/6000 system users to choose from the thousands of application programs that were originally developed for the UNIX operating system. This allows AIX users to capitalize on many application programs originally developed for other open systems. There is an application program to help users with just about anything they want to do. Some examples include accounting, computer-aided design, statistical analysis, financial modeling, word processing, desktop publishing, database management, electronic mail, animated computer graphics, and so on.

What about the operating system and device driver layers? The ability to run earlier UNIX operating system software is important for several reasons. Operating systems typically represent only a small fraction of the user's software investment; they can be upgraded easily without changing the user's view of the computer system. Further, a new operating system is usually necessary to allow users to have access to new features of the computer system not considered by the programmers of the old operating system. Of course, one of the primary purposes of the device driver layer is to allow the computer hardware to change without affecting compatibility with the operating system and application programs. This is done by changing the way a device driver interacts with the hardware without changing the way the device driver interacts with the operating system or application programs. The user is supplied with new device drivers to support pSeries and RS/6000 hardware.

Operating Systems

Few areas in information processing create more confusion and apprehension than the operating system. This section should help remove some of the mystery associated with the operating system used with the pSeries and RS/6000 systems.

AIX for the pSeries and RS/6000

IBM took the basic UNIX operating system and incorporated enhancements developed by other organizations (e.g., UC Berkeley), added many enhancements of their own, and developed their version called the Advanced Interactive eXecutive (AIX). An entire family of AIX operating system products was developed, made up of AIX operating system versions for the smaller personal computers, pSeries and RS/6000 computers, and the larger System/370 and System/390 family of mainframe computers. This open-system approach was a departure from IBM's proprietary systems such as that of the AS/400 minicomputer or the MVS operating system for IBM's S/370 and S/390 mainframes. The pSeries and RS/6000 and the associated version of the AIX operating system represent IBM's second-generation UNIX-based operating system and workstation/server. (The IBM RT System was the first.)

The AIX operating system for the pSeries and RS/6000 is a multitasking, multi user operating system adhering to industry standards. The base AIX operating system product itself provides all of the essential functions necessary to make up a complete computer system, but there are optional extensions to the AIX operating system that, when purchased and installed, become a part of the operating system. These extensions each add new functions to the AIX operating system. This building-block approach allows each user to select only the functions needed, minimizing software costs and required hardware resources.

The AIX operating system and its extensions perform all housekeeping tasks for the pSeries and RS/6000 and interact with users to do things such as starting application programs, changing passwords, erasing files, and so on. The base AIX operating system comes with command-driven user interfaces that require the user to type in somewhat cryptic commands. AIX also provides an industry-standard extension to the AIX operating system called CDE (for Common Desktop Environment) that provides an easier-to-use graphical user interface. The graphical user interfaces, along with the Systems Management Interface Tool (SMIT), browser-based management interface, and online documentation, provided as standard, make the pSeries and RS/6000 version of the AIX operating system easier to use than any of its previous versions. The AIX operating system maintains a high level of compatibility with earlier UNIX operating system versions and industry standards to provide compatibility with many application programs written for other open systems.

IBM has also added improvements such as more flexible disk management, improved security, and better data availability. Traditional UNIX development tools (such as the source code control system, subroutine libraries, and the Make command) are addressed as well as some newer tools (e.g., object-oriented programming and computer-aided software engineering products). The AIX operating system communications functions address traditional UNIX operating system communications (e.g., asynchronous ASCII protocol), current industry standards (e.g., TCP/IP and the network file system), and the IBM System Network Architecture (e.g., 3270 emulation and LU 6.2 protocols). Finally, personal computers can be attached to pSeries and RS/6000 systems in order to share disks, printers, data, and so forth.

Basically, IBM has started with the UNIX operating system base, incorporated enhancements made by many organizations, and added some new ideas, all without losing compatibility with industry standards (POSIX, SVID2, or Open Group). The AIX operating system is an open system, and IBM has stated its intention to evolve the AIX operating system to conform to new industry standards as they emerge. One organization that has a major influence on the development of AIX is the Open Group. The Open Group is a nonprofit consortium of computer vendors (including IBM, HP, Sun, and others) formed in 1996 by the merger of X/Open and the Open Software Foundation (OSF). The mission of the Open Group is to develop specifications and software for the open-system arena and make the resulting specifications and software available to computer vendors under fair and equitable licensing terms. In fact, it is the Open Group, through the use of a branding program, who determines whether one can call their operating system "UNIX." AIX is branded at the highest level, known as UNIX 98. The Open Group solicits members and nonmembers for submissions of concepts and software to solve a particular problem, then evaluates each submission and selects the best. This submission then becomes the Open Group-endorsed standard for the open-system environment. This process is designed to foster the development of vendor-neutral, open-system standards that many different computer vendors can implement in a compatible fashion. IBM has committed to support Open Group technologies and standards as they emerge in AIX.

AIX Version 3 was the level introduced with the first RS/6000 back in 1990. It has been through two major releases, (3.1 and 3.2), both of which are now unavailable. The current production version of AIX, which is version 4, is available at release level 3, and modification 3, designated AIX V4.3.3.

AIX Commonality on Intel Hardware

Late in 2000, a version of AIX was introduced that delivered on the promise of an earlier project known as Monterey (more on Monterey in the chapter on NUMA-Q). AIX Version 5.0 was made available for the PowerPC architecture as well as for the Intel 64-bit (IA-64) architecture. The first Intel microprocessor using this architecture is called Itanium. With this availability, the same application source code can be used to compile applications that run on the pSeries and RS/6000 as well as future systems from IBM and other hardware providers built on the IA-64 architecture. Check the companion Web site mentioned in the introduction of this book for the latest on AIX.

4

iSeries and AS/400e Computers

This chapter examines IBM's @server iSeries and AS/400 computer families. These systems are very popular mid-range business computers. We begin with the history then examine the hardware and software.

A Glance Backwards

On July 30, 1969, IBM executives from the entire company joined 1,200 IBM employees at their plant site in Rochester, Minnesota, to announce the System/3 computer shown in Figure 4.1. This system was the first computer to be totally developed at the Rochester location. Although only of historical interest today, the System/3 represented some significant advances in the technology of its time. For example, it introduced monolithic systems technology, which allowed engineers to package more circuitry in a smaller space, as well as a punch card one-third of normal size that held 20 percent more information. This was the first advancement in punch-card technology in over 40 years!

Figure 4.1.   IBM System/3.

The Rochester plant, which became a full IBM division in November of that year, was subsequently given the task of developing a "low-end" computer family. One System/3, fondly named "Old Reliable," ran faithfully until it was shut down in September 1973. When it was finally retired, its meter showed that it had run for 15,377.97 hours, representing more run time than any other system in existence.

The System/32, shown in Figure 4.2, was the next member of the family. It was announced in January 1975 and featured direct keyboard data entry and a display that could present up to six rows of text 40 characters long. The System/32 had up to 32K of memory and up to 13 MB of fixed-disk storage.

The System/34 computer, announced in April 1977, was the first system truly designed to manage multiple (local and remote) workstations (i.e., terminals and printers), each located up to 5,000 feet away from the computer. This allowed it to perform tasks for up to eight local users simultaneously. The System/34, shown in Figure 4.3, provided up to 256K of memory and 13 MB of fixed disk.

Figure 4.2. IBM System/32.

Figure 4.3. IBM System/34.

Next came the System/38, announced in October 1978. This rep-resented a divergence from its S/3X predecessors, offering a new ar-chitecture optimized for application development productivity. The System/38, shown in Figure 4.4, could support up to 32 MB of memory, 14 GB of disk storage, and 256 local workstations.

Figure 4.4. IBM System/38.

Once again, building on the architectural base of the System/34, the first System/36 was announced in May 1983 (Figure 4.5). It grew to support up to 7 MB of main memory, 1.4 GB of disk storage, and 72 local workstations. Other models of the System/36, varying in processing power and capacity, were announced over time. Collectively the System/3, System/32, System/34, System/36, and System/38 are known as the System/3X family of computers.

The last S/36 model (the 5363) has been enhanced and renamed the IBM AS/Entry system in 1987. IBM has provided future enhancements to the AS/Entry products. This means that they are vital to IBM's mid-range product strategy.

On June 20, 1988, IBM unveiled the AS/400 family of products. The AS/400 has close architectural ties with System/38 while in most cases providing application program compatibility with both the System/36 and the System/38. Then in October of 2000, IBM changed

Figure 4.5. IBM System/36.

the name of all its server lines and the AS/400 family became the IBM @server iSeries family. The remainder of this chapter focuses on the new IBM @server iSeries systems, the most current AS/400 models, and the latest version of the OS/400 operating system.

What Makes Up an iSeries or AS/400 Computer System?

The IBM @server iSeries and AS/400 family of products represents IBM's latest generation of midsize business computing systems. Like their predecessors, the System/3X family, they are multiuser computer systems, meaning that a single computer can interact with more than one user at a time. In developing the iSeries and AS/400 systems, designers drew from the ease-of-use features of the System/36, combined these with the advanced architecture and productivity of the System/38, and then added new functions. In addition to the many application programs developed directly for execution on the iSeries and AS/400, many of the application programs developed for the System/36 and System/38 computers can be migrated to and used on the latest models by applying the migration tools available.

Many users have no conception of what equipment makes up the computer system they use daily. Fortunately, they do not have to—just as it is not necessary to understand an engine to drive a car. However, it is helpful to have a fundamental view of what general elements make up a complete system. Figure 4.6 shows the components of a very simple iSeries system configuration. The heart of the system is the system unit, which contains the "brain" that runs the computer programs and controls all activities. In the largest systems, the system unit has been split into a processor/memory complex and an I/O complex. People interact with the computer system through terminals (or personal computers acting as terminals) that display computer information and allow for keyboard entry. The terminal shown on the left side of the figure is the

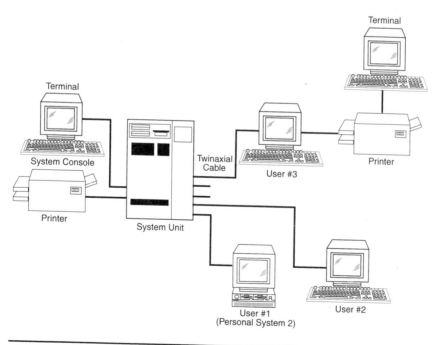

Figure 4.6. Components of a simple AS/400 system.

system console. The system console is a specially designated terminal used by the system operator to manage the day-to-day operations of the computer system. The other terminals are for general-purpose use. The printers shown in the figure are used to generate reports, documents, graphs, and the like. A printer can be a workstation used to fill the needs of specific user(s), or all users can share it. Both terminals and printers were initially attached to the system unit via twin-axial cable (or twinax), typically laid in the building's walls or ceiling. In today's environment, the terminals (personal computers) and printers are attached through many other media including radio communications and telephone wiring.

Meet the iSeries and AS/400 Family

As of this writing, twelve basic computers form the core of the iSeries and AS/400e family: the entry Model 150, available in both general-purpose and server configurations; the Model 250, which expands the growth possibilities for the entry-level customer; the Model 170 server versions with seven processor options; Model 270 server versions with four processor options; the six server Models 720, 730, 740, 820, 830, and 840; the dedicated Domino Servers Models 170D, 270D, and 820D; and the custom application servers SB1, SB2, and SB3. The Domino Servers and the custom application servers are special cases either through hardware constraints or software constraints of previously identified models.

IBM has chosen to separately classify the 270, 820, 830, 840, the dedicated Domino servers 270D and 820D and the third-tier servers SB2 and SB3 as iSeries 400 EServers. The "i" in iSeries 400 stands for intelligent integration, featuring open systems functions which are built-in to the operating system and pretested for reliable, turnkey function. The integrated functions include web servers (IBM HTTP server and Apache server), Web application server (WebSphere Standard Edition), Java Virtual Machine (JVM), database (IBM DB2 Universal database for AS/400), communications (TCP/IP), OS/400 PASE, e-business security, and Linux in the future. This intelligent integration enables businesses to deploy solutions faster, with greater reliability, and lower cost of ownership while providing superior performance across a wide range of e-business applications based on industry standards. The new iSeries systems as a group offer new tools for managing e-business, application flexibility, innovative technology, and leading edge server performance. The microprocessors used in iSeries systems are based on copper interconnect and silicon on insulator technologies, which are innovations in the semiconductor industry. These technologies result in denser packages, lower power consumption, and higher performance. Also implemented in these systems is memory switching technology with switch speeds up to 36 GB per second. High Speed Links on these systems allow data transfer between I/O devices and other systems at rates up to 1 GB per second. The iSeries intelligent integration of these technologies allows businesses to benefit from enterprise class computing without the "enterprise size" IT support staff.

The iSeries architecture features a flexible operating environment that concurrently runs any combination of applications originally designed for the AS/400, UNIX, Linux (in the future), Windows, Domino, or Java environments. When that flexibility is combined with the iSeries workload management capabilities, logical partitioning (LPAR), and the integration of other xSeries systems, the iSeries enables businesses to run several diverse application environments on one physical machine. Choices are provided with regard to whether a business should expand an existing server farm, maintain the existing server farm, or consolidate server footprints on the iSeries for simplified management, increased availability, or lower total cost of ownership. The iSeries also offers businesses the freedom to grow without disruption through Capacity Upgrade on Demand features on the Model 840. These features enable a customer to activate immediate incremental processing power non-disruptively, when it is needed, and pay for it only when initiated.

The AS/400e server 150 continues to use the same packaging and has received some additional capabilities in the software that is available. The AS/400e server 250 expands the performance and the I/O capabilities available in the entry-level price range. The Model 170 has a lower-performance entry-point processor, and also a two-way increased performance high-end processor. The Model 270 extends the midrange offering of the Model 170 in performance, memory, and I/O capacity while offering processing performance capability needed to address compute intensive applications.

The six server Models 720, 730, 740, 820, 830, and 840 provide increased server performance and a base interactive performance level of 35, 70, and 120 CPW, respectively, and can be featured to support a significantly larger interactive workload. The Model 840 extends the N-way configuration to twenty-four processors, 96,000 MB of main storage, and eighteen terabytes of DASD. The three Domino dedicated servers Models 170D, 270D, and 820D provide specially tuned Domino environments.

The number of steps that may be taken from the base interactive performance to the maximum offered by a particular processor varies with the processor. In no case can the maximum client/server processor CPW performance value be exceeded when using the featured processor in interactive mode.

The capability to feature the amount of interactive performance available on each of the 720, 730, 740, 820, 830, and 840 servers allows them to support the ISV preload environment previously provided by the AS/400e custom mixed-mode server Models S20-ISV, S30-ISV, and S40-ISV. Upgrades from the previous custom mixed-mode server models to the V4R5 8XX servers are supported. The custom mixed-mode software packages continue to be provided by J. D. Edwards, Software Systems Associates, Intentia International's Movex V10.5, and International Business Systems (IBS), as well as others. The preload of the above business partner software packages continue to be offered on the AS/400e servers 170 and 270.

The custom application servers SB1, SB2, and SB3 are a main storage, DASD, and other-I/O-device-constrained versions of the eight-way, twelve-way, and twenty-four-way processor versions of the 740, 830, and 840 servers specifically tuned to provide high performance in the compute-intensive environment required by many multitiered computing environments. The SB1, SB2, and SB3 are intended to be used as SAP R3 application servers to a separate second-tier server.

For those unfamiliar with the AS/400e server Models 150, 170, 720, 730, and 740, the authors refer the reader to the nineth edition of the book, *Exploring IBM AS/400 Computers*.

Figure 4.7 contains a photograph of the AS/400e series family. The "e" in the model names for these systems signifies that the sys-

Figure 4.7. AS/400 V4R5 family showing (from left-rear) I/O Tower, Model 840 and 830; (from left front) models 820, 270, and 250.

tems are capable of supporting the electronic business environment. This means that the user may establish a storefront on the Web and conduct business with the assurance, for both user and customer, that any and all transactions are secure and private.

An AS/400 system can be used as a centralized system shared by a collection of users (i.e., an interactive environment) or as a server offering resources to others in a client/server network (i.e., a client/server environment). In the case of the 720, 730, 740, 820, 830, and 840, each of the processors can be configured with varying levels of interactive capability. The amount of interactive capability varies with the model and processor from a small fraction of the processor's computing power to 100 percent. Another difference for these models is that no degradation in performance occurs in either client/server or interactive performance before the full rated capacity of the selected processor or interactive feature is exhausted. The relationship between client/server performance and interactive performance is simple. Processor performance rating minus interactive performance being used equals client/server performance available. The capability to configure a server processor with interactive capability means that the user can optimize the system for either general-purpose environments (accessed through non-intelligent terminals) or server environments (accessed through other computers in a network).

The two fastest processors in the Model 820, all processors in the models 830 and 840 are built from a new technology Silicon-on-insulator using copper-interconnect wiring. Copper-interconnect wiring reduces the resistance of the interconnections on the chip, resulting in lower power dissipation. Silicon-on-insulator reduces the junction capacitance of the transistors, providing about a thirty percent increase in the performance of the circuits on the chip. The AS/400 is the first system family in which these new technologies are being delivered.

Those models containing multiple processors (four or greater) include the capability to support logical partitioning, which provides the opportunity for server consolidation. Logical partitioning within a single AS/400 system, provides the capability for multiple independent partitions (each with its own processor(s), memory, and disks) within a single, symmetric, multiprocessing AS/400. Each logical partition behaves as if it were a separate, independently functioning AS/400 server. In these cases, each server could for example support a different National Language or be dedicated to a unique process. On the largest AS/400 Model 840, up to twenty-four partitions are supported.

A Glance Ahead

In the near future, IBM has announced that a partition can be formed on a fractional processor, increasing the number of total partitions beyond the number of processors present.

The server consolidation can be accomplished with low risk and high availability (AS/400 availability is at 99.9%) and is further enhanced by integrated cluster resource management, the implementation of data and application resiliency, and check point restart software. These new capabilities acting in combination with the already existing high-speed opticonnect and remote cluster nodes for disaster tolerance increase the AS/400e availability to 100%.

Inside iSeries and AS/400 Systems

Many elements provide the functions and performance of iSeries and AS/400 computers. In this section, we look at some of the things that make these systems unique.

Hardware Architecture Overview

The underlying arrangement and interconnection of a computer system's electrical components is called its hardware architecture. This architecture is the fundamental structure upon which all system functions are built and has the largest effect on how the computer system will behave. A basic understanding of the iSeries and AS/400 system architecture (depicted in Figure 4.8) makes it possible to compare these computers with other systems and to understand important aspects of system performance and capacity.

The core of the iSeries and AS/400 computers (as in all computers) is the system processor (shown near the center of the figure). The system processor is the circuitry that actually executes a computer program's instructions and does all the mathematical calculations. To review groupings of data, recall that the smallest piece of information (data) in the computer is called a bit. Bits are grouped into bytes (8 bits), half words (16 bits), full words (32 bits), and double words (64 bits) inside the computer. These groupings form the computer's representation of numbers, letters of the alphabet, and instructions in a program. These system processors move information around one double word (64 bits) at a time. Since much of a computer's time is spent moving information around, the double-word organization helps improve overall system performance.

Other bits inside the system processor are used to uniquely identify (address) storage and input/output devices (e.g., a disk unit) within the computer system. iSeries and AS/400 system processors group 64 bits together to form a unique address. This 64-bit addressing provides 18,446,744 trillion (2^{64}) unique addresses, which is more than any other IBM computer system—from PCs to the largest S/390 computers. This is more than enough address space for today's midsize computer environment (and even for the foreseeable future). In fact, the largest iServer systems and servers today are just capable of using

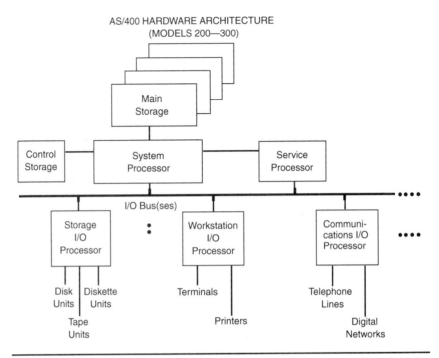

Figure 4.8. Block diagram of AS/400 hardware architecture used in all single-processor AS/400 systems.

just under *nineteen* trillion of those addresses. This shows the kind of growth inherent in the architecture.

The "memory," or main storage (shown at the top of the figure), provides a workspace for the system processor. Since much of a computer's time is spent moving information to and from main storage, the speed of main storage can be a limiting factor for the overall performance of any computer system. The speed of storage is measured by the time it takes to respond to a request to store or recall information, or the cycle time. The main storage cycle time for iSeries and AS/400 computers varies depending on the model. The shorter the cycle time, the better the system performance. The largest systems can have up to 96,000 MB of main storage. The main storage in all AS/400 systems provides error detection and error correction. These main-storage error functions work to protect the important integrity of user information in the computer system.

All iSeries and AS/400 system processors also use cache memory to help increase the effective cycle time of main storage. A cache is a small and high-speed memory area that sits between the processor and main storage. The idea is to keep the information most likely to be needed next in cache to avoid the time delay associated with main storage. iSeries and AS/400 systems have data and instruction caches on the processor to accelerate performance when accessing information/program instructions (respectively).

Another important part of the system architecture is the System Licensed Internal Code (SLIC). SLIC is a set of extremely simple instructions (never seen by the computer programmer or user) that are directly performed by the electronic circuits within the system processor. The SLIC instruction layer exists just below the Independent Machine Interface. The Independent Machine Interface (MI) is the lowest level of programming perceived by application programmers. All user program instructions are automatically converted into a series of these SLIC instructions, which are then executed by the system processor.

The larger systems, starting with the Model 270 and continuing through the Model 840 use a High Speed Link to connect to the I/O functions. The High Speed Link (HSL) is also used to connect system to system at a processor to processor level and to migrate the I/O devices from older systems. The HSL increases the overall bandwidth of the I/O connections to the processor complex, increases the amount of I/O capacity of the systems, and enables the migration of the older model system units to the 8XX models. This migration is accomplished by converting the old system unit to a HSL attached I/O unit.

The input/output processors (shown at the bottom of the figure) are responsible for managing any devices attached to the system. Each of these specialized processors has independent responsibilities and performs tasks in coordination with the system processor. A computer that has multiple processors working together with the system processor has what is called multiprocessor architecture. The advantage of having multiple processors performing work simultaneously is that more work can be done in a given period of time. For example, the workstation (I/O) processor manages the detailed processing associated with the multiple terminals and printers attached to the system, allowing the system processor to concentrate on doing more productive work for the user. The same is true of the other specialized I/O processors, such as the storage I/O processor that manages disk, diskette, and tape devices attached to the AS/400 system. The I/O processors communicate with the system processor over an I/O bus (called the PCI bus) which is a group of wires that carry information very quickly from one area to another inside the computer system. As indicated in the figure, some systems have a single I/O bus, whereas others have multiple I/O buses (today's implementations have 19 I/O buses maximum). Because only one information transfer can occur on any one bus at any one time, systems with multiple buses have the advantage of allowing overlapping transfers between I/O processors and the system processor or main storage. Therefore, multiple buses contribute to the overall performance of larger systems.

Various controllers and adapters plug into physical slots in each of the packages used to provide electrical connections to the bus. In addition to I/O processors, a service processor (shown in the upper right of the figure) is built into every system. It is responsible for starting the system and constantly monitoring the status of the entire computer. It interacts with the system operator through the control panel and helps with such things as system-fault isolation, error detection, and error reporting. It is like having a built-in service technician who watches over things with relentless consistency.

All iSeries and AS/400 systems employ multiprocessor architecture in that they have a system processor and multiple specialized processors (e.g., workstation and I/O processors) to handle specific tasks. However, larger models (e.g., Models 170, 270, 720, 730, 740, 820, 830, and 840) employ multiple-system processors cooperatively executing a single copy of the operating system (OS/400), thus appearing to be a single large processor, or in cases requiring high availability, multiple copies of the operating system may be executed. This multiple-system-processor architecture is called the N-way multiprocessor architecture (where "N" is replaced by the number of processors), also referred to as the Symmetric

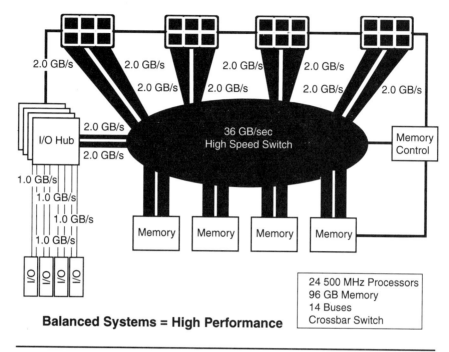

2.0 GB/s   2.0 GB/s   2.0 GB/s   2.0 GB/s
2.0 GB/s   2.0 GB/s   2.0 GB/s   2.0 GB/s

2.0 GB/s   36 GB/sec   Memory
I/O Hub   High Speed Switch   Control
2.0 GB/s

1.0 GB/s
1.0 GB/s
1.0 GB/s
1.0 GB/s

Memory   Memory   Memory   Memory

I/O   I/O   I/O   I/O

24 500 MHz Processors
96 GB Memory
14 Buses
Crossbar Switch

Balanced Systems = High Performance

Figure 4.9.   N-Way hardware architecture block diagram.

MultiProcessor (SMP) architecture. Figure 4.9 shows how N-way models are organized. (*Note:* All system processors share the same I/O buses, I/O processors, and main storage.) Symmetric multiprocessors process in parallel, sharing a task list. Each processor in an SMP set has its own data and instruction cache, and its own virtual storage view of the system. In the case of a query, each processor in the SMP group will process in parallel against a segment of disk storage to resolve the query.

In the high-availability environment mentioned above, separate processors or groups of processors must be assigned unique I/O groupings. Data may be shared among the processor groups using the OptiConnect function, and I/O functions can be switched between logical partitions. This high-availability environment is included in the definition of logical partitioning, but could also be defined by clustering unique systems or groupings of systems.

The Move from CISC to RISC

As we have seen, the system processor is the circuitry that actually executes a computer program's instructions and does all the mathematical calculations. Before 1995, all AS/400 systems processors were based on the CISC (Complex Instruction Set Computer) concept.

Although additional improvements could have been achieved with the CISC-based processor, the AS/400 and iSeries now use a RISC (Reduced Instruction Set Computer, pronounced "risk") base because RISC provides extended future growth, is mainstream and strategic, can be optimized for commercial usage, and offers several advantages at a complete system level—which involves more than chips. RISC also better enables an optimizing compiler as well as simplifying the instruction-decode function.

Auxiliary Storage

Auxiliary storage, commonly used to keep data and program information in all computers, is an inexpensive way to retain and later access information. The information kept on auxiliary storage can easily be modified or kept unchanged over long periods of time as an archive. Because all auxiliary storage is nonvolatile, the information stored remains intact whether the computer is turned on or off. The iSeries and AS/400 systems use four types of auxiliary storage: diskette, disk, optical libraries, and tape.

Diskette Storage

Diskettes are a portable magnetic storage medium that can be used to record and later retrieve computer information via a diskette unit. The diskettes consist of a flexible disk with a magnetic surface permanently enclosed in a square protective outer jacket, as shown in Figure 4.10.

One of the primary functions of diskettes is to provide portable storage, allowing for the transfer of programs and data between computers. To this end, all similarly configured iSeries and AS/400 computer systems can freely exchange programs and data via diskettes. Also, information on System/3X diskettes can be freely exchanged with a properly configured computer. As a result of their small capacity, diskettes have a decreasing usage on today's systems.

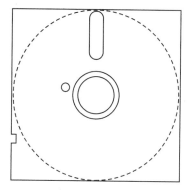

Figure 4.10. Diskette used with Application Systems.

Disk Storage

Another kind of auxiliary storage used with iSeries and AS/400 systems, is called disk storage units or Direct Access Storage Devices (DASDs). These are high-capacity magnetic storage devices commonly used in all types of computers from personal computers to large mainframe computer systems. The basic anatomy of a disk unit is shown in Figure 4.11. Disks consist of a drive mechanism with permanently installed metallic disks often called platters (because they are shaped like a dinner plate). These platters have a magnetic surface that can store information. The platters spin at a very high constant speed while the read/write heads record or detect information on the platters' surfaces. The arm that positions the read/write head is called the actuator. The read/write heads in disk units never actually touch the magnetic surface of the platter, but are positioned very close to that surface.

Optical Libraries

Optical libraries consist of arrays of optical disks associated with one or more optical disk read/write units. In some cases, the optical storage read/write units also have one or more conventional magnetic disk storage units associated with them to improve the write performance from a system perspective. The optical disks may be CD-ROM, WORM, or WMRM technology, each of which imposes different

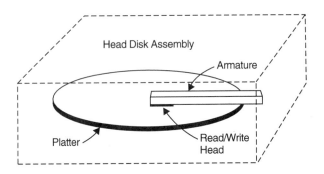

Figure 4.11. The anatomy of a disk unit.

requirements upon the read/write unit and upon the controller within the system. CD-ROM is an abbreviation for Compact Disk–Read Only Memory, and the technology presents digital data in a continuous serpentine path across the surface of the optical disk. WORM is an abbreviation for Write Once, Read Many. This technology presents data in circumferential paths across the surface of the optical disk. Circumferential paths are paths written along the circumference of the disk. Because the data will be written only once, this technology generally has the header embedded on the raw media, and a sector corresponds to the data content that can fit in the shortest circumferential track. WMRM, sometimes referred to as erasable optical disk technology, is an abbreviation for Write Many, Read Many and also presents data in circumferential paths across the surface of the optical disk. But previously written data must be erased before new data may be written to replace it, and it must follow the sectoring, header, trailer, and error-correction rules of magnetic-disk technology, including bad-track recovery and directory management.

Tape Storage

The last type of auxiliary storage to be covered is magnetic tape, or simply "tape." One primary purpose of tape is to provide a backup storage medium for information on the computer's disk storage. The low cost and high recording densities inherent in tape make it ideal for archiving information. Tape is also useful for distributing programs and transferring information from one computer system to another. Diskettes can be used for these same functions, but the higher storage capacity of tapes is preferred if you are dealing with a large amount of information. Tape storage consists of a long, flexible strip coated with magnetic material and rolled onto a reel or into a cartridge.

Storage Management

The methods used within a computer system to manage main storage and disk storage are collectively called the computer's storage management and are fundamental to the capabilities of the computer. Understanding the basics of this storage management provides insight into one of the unique features of iSeries and AS/400 computers when compared with traditional computer systems.

Figure 4.12 is a conceptual view of what the storage in iSeries and AS/400 computers looks like. All programs and information currently being used by the computer system must be contained in main storage that resides inside the computer's system unit. Main storage is relatively expensive and responds at very high speeds (compared to disk storage) when called on to provide or store information. Because main storage loses all information when the computer system is turned off, it is called volatile storage.

Disk storage is less expensive but cannot provide or store information as quickly as main storage. Disk storage is said to be nonvolatile because it does not lose its information when the power is turned off (or lost due to a power failure). As a result of this nonvolatility and

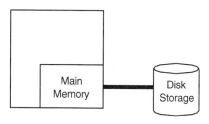

Figure 4.12. AS/400 main storage and fixed disk storage.

relatively low cost, disk storage is commonly used to hold all information that must be readily available to the computer. The disk storage may reside either inside the system unit or inside a separate box cabled to the system unit (as depicted in the figure).

When the computer is first turned on, information vital to an orderly startup and smooth operation is automatically copied from the disk to main storage. After normal system operation is established, users can begin to do their work. During the course of this work, users will start various computer programs. As each program is started, it is copied from the disk to main storage and then executed. Depending on the work being done, the computer programs manipulate various sets of data that are also loaded from the disk as needed. It does not take long to realize that the main storage in a computer can quickly become filled up with programs and data as the system is called upon to do more and more work.

In the earlier days of computing, the main storage size limited the amount of work a computer could manage at any one time. This restriction controlled the size of programs, the number of programs that could be run concurrently, the number of users who could share the system, and so on. In today's environment, a technique called virtual storage alleviates the need to squeeze all active programs and data into main storage. In computers that support virtual storage, the computer basically "fakes out" the computer programs and users and appears to have much more main storage than it actually has. iSeries and AS/400 systems provide a virtual storage size of 18 million TB (terabytes). Virtual storage therefore allows more programs, data, and users to be simultaneously active on the system than could be supported in real main storage.

Although virtual storage is a powerful system feature, the "swapping" between disk and main storage is processing overhead that can reduce the overall system performance. A little swapping does not appreciably hurt performance, but increased swapping does. When the swapping performed by a virtual storage system becomes excessive, the system is said to be "thrashing," or spending too much time swapping information between disk and main storage. Thrashing can be reduced by increasing the amount of main storage in the iSeries or AS/400 system through the installation of main-storage expansion options. Increasing the main storage in the system provides more room for programs and data, reducing the amount of virtual storage swapping. Thrashing can also be reduced through system management means such as rescheduling work for off-peak periods.

The virtual storage concept is implemented in many of today's computer systems to one degree or another. iSeries and AS/400 systems implement their virtual storage scheme through a concept called single-level storage. This simply means that in iSeries and AS/400 systems, no distinction is made between disk storage and main storage. All storage appears to be one homogeneous mass of main storage accessed in exactly the same way. This consistency provides for a simple and efficient virtual storage implementation that is the same for programs, data, temporary holding areas, and so forth. The simplicity of single-level storage results in a consistent and more-complete virtual storage system than most other implementations.

Another difference between iSeries and AS/400 storage management and that of conventional computer systems is its object-oriented access. With this concept, all programs, databases, documents, and so on, stored in iSeries and AS/400 computers are stored as independent entities called objects. Object-oriented access again provides the user and the programmer with a simple and consistent way of managing all programs and information in the system. Users can access an object by simply referring to its name. The iSeries and AS/400 security system will check to make sure that the user has authorization to use the object and that it is being used properly. This is called capability-based addressing. The system manages the complexities associated with the physical location and addressing of the information.

The iSeries and AS/400's implementation of single-level storage and capability-based addressing spreads information through various disk units in a way that optimizes storage efficiency. Objects provide consistency in the areas of security, usage, and systems management for all items stored on the computer. Objects can be organized into groups called libraries. A library (which is also an object) is analogous to a drawer in a file cabinet (or a subdirectory, for those familiar with personal computer disk management). To keep things organized a library might contain, for example, all programs related to the accounting function of a business. Because access to libraries can be restricted by the security system, a payroll database, for example, might be kept in a library separate from other business information for security reasons.

Hardware Data Compression

The disk adapters used in iSeries and the latest AS/400 models perform hardware disk compression to allow them to store more information than would otherwise be possible. The data is dynamically compressed/decompressed by the disk controller, independently of the system processor. The average compression ratio achieved is 2:1 (data is stored in one-half the space), with 4:1 attainable. Reliability of stored information remains protected (using RAID-5 and mirroring) in the compressed environment.

Hierarchical Storage Management

Hierarchical Storage Management (HSM) allows users to migrate data as it ages from fast (and expensive) disk devices to progressively lower-cost storage devices like compressed disk devices, optical devices, and tape devices. Yet, data stored on tape devices is accessed just like data residing on disk (though slower).

BRMS/400 is the application program that provides the foundation for HSM. BRMS/400 defines a new set of policies under which the user can determine when the different object types can be moved or migrated to the different levels of storage.

NetFinity for AS/400

NetFinity for AS/400 is a combination of the Integrated PC Server function and two software packages described below. The Integrated NetFinity Server function is basically a complete personal computer built on an AS/400 I/O adapter. The configuration of the adapters can be used to provide a firewall processor front-end interface to the AS/400, support for Lotus Notes/Domino, support for a Novell Netware interface, or to run Windows NT. (A firewall in the AS/ 400, is a processor function which isolates the users on the secure side of the system from the users on the Internet non-secure side of the system). Multiple Windows NT servers can exist within a single AS/400e server.

NetFinity for AS/400 (5716-SVA) is software that enables the movement of systems management tasks from end users to more-experienced system administrators. NetFinity contains an inventory server that collects hardware and software inventory information from the clients being managed and stores it in DB2/400 databases on the AS/400 server. This information is used to perform management tasks such as software distribution, distributed monitoring, and remote control. NetFinity enables the system administrator to perform remote control of the PC clients, allowing the identification and correction of potential problems before they impact business. NetFinity also provides a graphical interface to software distribution by defining custom reports for querying the hardware and software database, runs the reports and displays results, generates a node list for distributing software, and distributes the PC software. Other NetFinity capabilities include critical-file monitoring, workstation discovery, performance monitoring, activity scheduling, enhanced security, user profile data collection, alert management and processing, and problem analysis and correction.

NetFinity for AS/400 has two components: NetFinity Server for AS/400 (5716- SVA) is the server component, installed on the AS/400 servers and the central site system. NetFinity AS/400 Manager (5716-SVD) is a manager component installed on a PC connected to an AS/400 server in its workgroup. NetFinity Services for AS/400 (5716-SVE) contains the PC client code supporting NetFinity for AS/400. All the PCs to be managed within the enterprise must include this code, which performs the responses directed by the NetFinity Manager and NetFinity for AS/400 software. NetFinity Server for AS/400 includes an easy-to-use interface for setting up proactive resource monitors and alert conditions on the clients. Client alerts notify the manager when conditions are met, such as changes to critical files, the start or end of a critical process, or performance and capacity statistics. Administrators can view a snapshot of the screen, start a command-line session, transfer files, browse information in the desktop management interface, and view current hardware and software configurations on remote clients.

In order to support remote control of Windows NT Server on the Integrated PC Server, NetFinity requires a local managing workstation for the remote server, control of the remote console keyboard/mouse, the capability to inventory the software and hardware, and to perform software distribution through the AS/400 using Managed System Services (MSS). PC systems supported as clients are Windows 3.1, Windows 95/98, Windows NT, and OS/2.

Opticonnect/400 Systems

An Opticonnect/400 is a high-speed, fiber optic link that can be used to connect multiple iSeries or AS/400 systems together. Prior to Opticonnect/400, when the performance of a system was fully tapped, additional processing power could be obtained only by replacing the existing computer system with a more-powerful model.

Opticonnect/400 systems allow the interconnection of the existing system with one or more additional iSeries or AS/400 computer systems to add computing power. This interconnection is referred to as loosely coupled computing and is similar to the distributed computing environment for the server models, except that the sharing is performed at a much higher level in the individual systems. The higher the level at which sharing is performed, the lower the complexity introduced in the execution of the sharing function.

Each system participating in the sharing function loses one I/O bus to the sharing function. Figure 4.13 shows the sharing function for three systems. The clustering is performed including one of the fiber optic buses from each system (AS/400 models 720, 730, and 740, plus iSeries models 820, 830, and 840 only) in the system cluster. The fiber optic bus is connected to the other systems by using an optical bus adapter in a bus expansion unit. One optical bus adapter must be used for each system to be included in the system cluster. A maximum of 128 system nodes can be included in an Opticonnect/400 system. Data and applications may be shared across Opticonnect/400 systems using the distributed data-management facilities of the OS/400 operating system. With the availability of the 1063-Mbps (megabits per second) fiber optic bus adapter on these systems, the latency and performance of this connection is improved by better then seven times.

iServer and AS/400 Software

As with other types of computers, iSeries and AS/400 systems use several different types of software, each diverse in function and purpose. Below is an overview of this software.

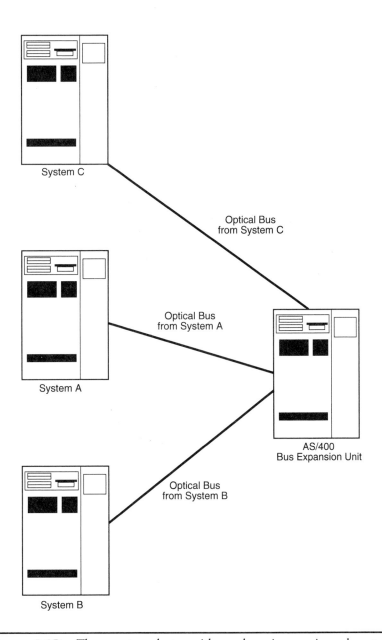

Figure 4.13. Three system cluster with one bus given up in each system to connect to the expansion tower.

Types of Software—A Model

The basic categories of real software used in iSeries and AS/400 systems can be understood through the simple software model (Figure 4.14). Three basic software layers are commonly used with these systems: the application program layer, the operating system layer, and the System Licensed Internal Code (SLIC) layer. Although each software layer performs a completely different job, all three work closely together to perform useful tasks for the user. Some special-purpose programs do not fit neatly into any of these three categories, but the majority of software commonly used does. For now, we will briefly examine each of the three layers in our software model.

Application Programs

The top software layer in the software model is the application program layer (highlighted in Figure 4.15). The programs in this layer

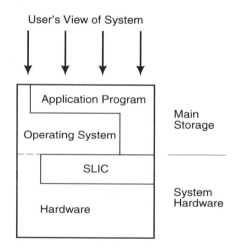

Figure 4.14. Conceptual software model of the basic software structure. The three layers of the software model work together to perform useful work for the user.

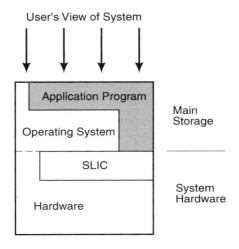

Figure 4.15. The application program software layer of the model, highlighted above, defines the particular tasks the computer is performing for the user.

apply computer system to a specific task (e.g., payroll or accounting) and thus are called application programs. They actually perform the task for which the user purchased the computer, whereas the other two layers play important support roles. The "User's View" arrows in the figure indicate that the user usually interacts with the application program layer and less frequently with the operating system. By working closely with the other software layers, the application program processes the various keystrokes made by the user and responds by displaying information on the computer's display or some other output device.

Programs written for System/3X computers can be either directly executed or migrated to iSeries and AS/400 systems. This allows AS users to capitalize on the thousands of application programs available for these popular business systems. There is an application program that can help users with just about anything they wish to do. Some more-common functions application programs perform in the business environment are accounting, financial modeling, word processing, database management, electronic mail, and Web site hosting.

Operating Systems

The next layer in our software model is called the operating system (highlighted in Figure 4.16). The operating system must manage the hardware resources of the computer system and perform tasks under the control of application programs and keyboard commands typed by the user. The application program can rely on the operating system to perform many of the detailed *housekeeping* tasks associated with the internal workings of the computer. Thus, the operating system is said to provide the *environment* in which application programs execute. Operating systems also accept commands directly from the user to do such things as copying files and changing passwords. The operating system must also manage the system variables used for tailoring the major types of objects supported by the system, such as programs, files (databases, print, display, etc.), and communications protocols, and must provide national language support. OS/400 is the operating system used on all iSeries and AS/400 computers.

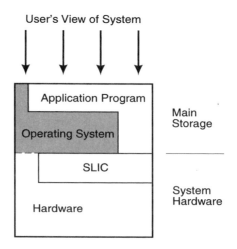

Figure 4.16. The operating system software layer of the model, highlighted above, provides the environment in which the application program(s) run.

SLIC Instructions

The third and final layer of software in our software model is called the System Licensed Internal Code (SLIC) layer (highlighted in Figure 4.17). SLIC (as previously described) is a set of highly specialized programs written by the manufacturer of a computer and never tampered with by the computer operator or users. The set of SLIC instructions in iSeries and AS/400 computers is embedded deeply within the computer system and is therefore considered to be part of the computing machine itself rather than part of a program running on the machine. Unlike application programs or operating systems, only other programs use SLIC. That is, SLIC never interacts directly with the user or the programmer; it exists only to help application programs and the operating system perform their tasks. SLIC instructions also help shield application programs from the hardware specifics of computers, allowing for evolutionary product improvements without sacrificing application program compatibility.

It is the particularly rich SLIC layer in iSeries and AS/400 that helps set its architecture apart from those of more-conventional com-

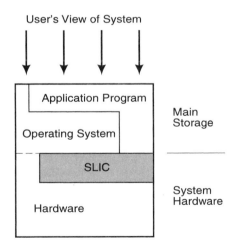

Figure 4.17. The SLIC software layer of the model, highlighted above, directly controls the hardware elements of the system and shields application programs and the operating system from hardware details.

puters. The built-in database, single-level storage, object-oriented architecture, and other features are all designed into the SLIC layer making them part of the machine itself. This results in highly efficient, consistent, and easy-to-use implementations of these functions.

How iSeries and AS/400 Software Layers Are Different

One of the basic differences between iSeries and AS/400 computers as compared to more traditional computer systems can be seen by examining the software layers. Figure 4.18 shows the three software layers of our model (application, operating system, and SLIC) in a more detail. The figure shows the traditional software layers side by

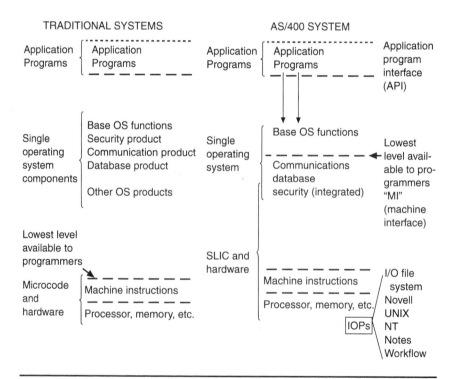

Figure 4.18. The AS/400's software architecture differs from that of more traditional systems. Implementing more function in the SLIC layer and providing a one-piece operating system results in improved efficiency, consistency, and simplicity.

side with those of the iSeries and AS/400. The first difference is between where the various software functions reside in the layers. In the traditional system, functions such as security, database, and communications reside in the operating system layer (usually made up of a collection of separately purchased operating system products). Using this traditional approach, each operating system product must be installed and maintained separately, requiring a highly skilled individual (called a systems programmer) to support this kind of system.

The Independent Machine Interface (MI) is the function of the iSeries and AS/400 system architecture which has allowed the system to be reinvented from a hardware aspect while compatibly supporting the wide range of applications which have been written to execute on the system. Since the Application Program layer and Operating System layers interface directly to the MI and cannot perceive changes under the MI, the iSeries and AS/400 designers have the freedom to change processor architecture from 32 bit to 64 bit, from CISC to RISC, etc. as long as the SLIC code on top of the hardware preserves the MI view of the system. New operating system functions can be added to the system as needed as long as the hardware view of the MI through the SLIC software layer is preserved.

In the iSeries and AS/400 approach, much of the basic database, security, and other functions are built into the SLIC layer. This results in overall system performance improvement, because SLIC implementations are in general more efficient by nature of their proximity to the hardware. The OS/400 operating system provides all of its functions in a single product, eliminating the need for the operator to install, tailor, and manage the multiple operating system components in traditional operating systems. The operator is also relieved of the need to insure that each of the components of the operating system continues to work with the other components as new versions are shipped at different times. The price of this simplicity is that all OS/400 functions are there whether needed or not, whereas in a traditional operating system, the user can select only the functions needed at a given time.

Another basic difference lies in the way a programmer "sees" the different systems. With the traditional system, system functions such as database management or security reside in the operating system and can therefore be modified by a systems programmer. This gives the systems programmer more flexibility in customizing the computer system at the expense of more complexity. With iSeries and AS/400 systems, ease of use and efficiency are gained at the price of some flexibility. For example, because the database functions are built into the SLIC instructions, they cannot be modified. If the programmers want to change how the database is managed there are some things they simply cannot do. In a traditional systems environment, the database functions are not part of the operating system but are purchased as a separate component, such as Oracle, Sybase, or Informix. Thus other systems provide a choice that is not available in OS/400.

OS/400

Operating System/400, commonly called OS/400, is a multiuser operating system exclusively used with all iSeries and AS/400 computer systems. It works closely with SLIC instructions imbedded in the systems to implement the database, security, single-level storage, and so on that are basic to iSeries and AS/400 architecture. Its extensive database and communications support allows these systems to manage large amounts of information and to participate in many communications configurations. Available application development tools improve the productivity of programmers for those writing their own custom application programs.

Although OS/400 offers the user complex and sophisticated features, many things have been done to make OS/400 easier to use. One of the ease-of-use enhancements is the uniting of the OS/400 and the Windows 95/Windows NT 5.0 desktop to provide a new graphical interface for users who are familiar with the Windows interface. Other OS/400 items that directly address ease of use include automatic configuration of devices and table-driven customization.

Extensive help and online (computer-based) documentation is provided to reduce the need to go to reference manuals when the user needs more information. Online education using CD-ROMs is built into OS/400, allowing users to learn how to use the system while sitting in front of their terminal.

In addition to performing tasks under the direct control of the user, OS/400 can perform tasks under direct control of an application program, which can issue OS/400 commands through the OS/400. There is a defined protocol for passing information directly between the application program and OS/400 with no user interaction required. Often, OS/400 subsequently calls on the routines of the SLIC instructions to effect the desired action.

OS/400 provides multiple application programming interfaces to maintain compatibility with programs written for System/36, System/38, and, of course, AS/400 and iSeries systems. The OS/400 application-programming interface provides some new capabilities not found in earlier operating systems, such as the Structured Query Language (SQL) method of dealing with databases. OS/400 provides online education facilities and online help to assist users during interaction with the operating system. If a user gets stuck on some operating system screen, pressing the Help key causes some help text to appear on the screen. The particular help text shown depends on where the cursor was on the screen when the Help key was pressed; that is, the text will address the particular item at which the cursor was positioned. This is called contextual help.

OS/400 Upgrades

Just as with the hardware, IBM has continued to improve the Operating System, OS/400. The changes in OS/400 through the most recent releases have been oriented to maintain compatibility to the requirements of modern applications and to enable the iSeries and AS/400 systems to be used as servers for e-business in an Internet related environment. The following information provides a summary introduction to those improvements.

OS/400 and Modern Applications

OS/400 provides DCE Base Services/400 to support the Distributed Computer Environment as defined in Open Software foundation DCE Version 1.2.2. The code provided by the OSF for DCE has been enhanced to provide the feel and look of AS/400 with improved reliability, availability, and serviceability to make it consistent with other AS/400 products.

The relational database DB2, has been enhanced to provide the characteristics which qualify it to be identified as a Universal Database. The enhanced characteristics include complex object support, DataLink data types, User Defined Types, and User Defined Functions.

The client Access family of products provides AS/400-to-Windows desktop connectivity and function. Support is available for Windows 95, Windows 98, and Windows NT with both server and client platform capability. This support is functional in environments with TCP/IP and does not require SNA support.

Advanced Search algorithms like Encoded Vector Indexing improve database query performance for data warehouse, and data mining applications.

Support for Java, JavaBeans, and Threads enable your modern applications to realize the full performance capabilities available from the emergence of those programming techniques. In addition, the San Francisco project holds promise to alter the future direction of programming toward frameworks and reusable software modules.

OS/400 and e-business

Cryptography is supported both in hardware and software with offerings for 40, 56, and 128 bit encryption to protect the privacy of both company and customer data.

Digital Certificate Manager is provided to allow an iSeries or AS/400 system to serve as an Internet/intranet certificate authority, sign client and server certificates, distribute client certificates via a Web browser, and provide support for MD5 and SHA-1 hash algorithms.

Hash algorithms are mathematical procedures used to search through large volumes of information to match a specific requirement. MD5 and SHA-1 are two popular hash algorithms used for that purpose.

WebSphere Application Server provides a run time environment for Java servlets. WebSphere leverages Java to dynamically extend server functions to run in the context of the server process and to enable the "write-once use everywhere" concept.

Websphere Commerce Suite integrates the separate offerings of Net.Data, Net.Commerce, and so on into a single product which can be used to set up a Web site, build a store front, and access database information. NetQuestion as a search engine has been absorbed into the WebSphere Commerce Suite offering. Commerce Suite continues the usage of Lightweight Directory Access Protocol (LDAP) for directory services.

5

---

zSeries and S/390 Computers

This chapter provides an overview of IBM's most powerful line of business computers, the @server zSeries and S/390 families. It also examines the continually evolving capabilities of these systems in the age of e-business.

A Glance Backwards

In the 1950s, IBM helped shape the fledgling computer industry with a line of computers—with names like the 650, the 701, and the 305 RAMAC—based on vacuum tubes (Figure 5.1). (The 305 RAMAC, shown in Figure 5.2, provided the first disk storage in the industry.) During the decade of the 1950s, IBM enhanced these products and continued development of other computer systems—each uniquely designed to address specific applications and to fit within narrow price ranges.

This undisciplined proliferation of unique and incompatible computer systems caused confusion, even within IBM's own marketing, service, and software development organizations. The lack of "compatibility" among these systems also made it difficult for customers to migrate to new generations of IBM computers.

Figure 5.1. Vacuum tube rack used in the Model 701.

Figure 5.2. IBM 305 RAMAC computer system.

In 1961, a corporate task force (code-named "SPREAD" to indicate a wide scope) assembled at a Connecticut motel to define a new family of mutually compatible, general-purpose computers. The task force's final report recommended building a new series of computer systems spanning a wide range of price and performance. IBM's senior management accepted the recommendation just a week later, and a new development project was launched.

The first task undertaken by the development team was to define a set of rules—termed an architecture—to which a group of five computers would conform. This architectural-definition step was the key to ensuring that all five computer systems would be compatible with one another—a first for IBM. The architecture was completed and documented by the fall of 1962.

After defining the architecture, the development team turned to the task of simultaneously designing the five different models that made up the family. Enhanced core memory and a new Solid Logic Technology (SLT) improved performance and reliability. Finally, on April 7, 1964, IBM held a press conference, with over 200 editors and writers in attendance, to announce the IBM System/360 family of computers (Figure 5.3). The "360" in the name referred to all points of a compass to denote the universal applicability, wide range of performance and price, and the "whole company" scope of the development effort.

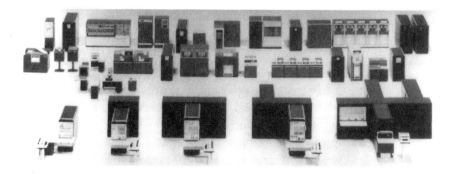

Figure 5.3. The IBM System/360 family of computer systems (mainframes foreground).

Although the System/360 architecture remained unchanged for six years, just six months after its introduction, IBM executives began to plan for systems that would exploit the emerging monolithic circuit. By the end of 1965, a draft document defining a new family of computer systems, called "NS" for "new systems," was complete. The new systems were to be based on monolithic circuit technology and an extended System/360 architecture to be called System/370.

In June 1970, IBM announced the System/370 Models 155 and 166. The System/370 architecture preserved upward compatibility with application programs written for the System/360 architecture. (That is, applications written to run on System/360 could also run on System/370 systems, but those written for System/370 would not execute on the older systems.)

During the development of the System/370 family, IBM recognized the need to expand the amount of main storage (often referred to as memory or central storage) available to application programs. This need led to the development of a second wave of System/370 computers that implemented a new concept called virtual memory. The virtual memory concept used a level of storage address translation to increase the amount of storage perceived available by application programs. That is, virtual memory made computer systems seem to have much more main storage than they actually did. Virtual memory was publicly announced in August 1972, along with System/370 Models 158 and 168 (Figure 5.4), replacing the original System/370 Models 155 and 166.

Models 158 and 168 brought the multiprocessing configuration to the System/370 family. With multiprocessing, two or more processors housed in a single computer system cooperate to execute available work. By the end of 1976, the addition of the Models 125 and 115 brought the number of announced System/370 models to 17.

Prompted by the still-growing need of users for main storage fueled by the increase in interactive processing (in which users hold a dialog with the computer), the System/370 product line was split into two compatible lines: the 30XX series of large systems and the 43XX series of mid-range systems (Figure 5.5).

In 1981, the main storage addressability of the 30XX series was quadrupled (up to 64 MB) by exploiting some extra addressing bits available but not used in the System/370 architecture. Additional main storage support came with the System/370 Extended Architecture (370-XA), announced in 1981 and first shipped in 1983. The 370-XA

Figure 5.4. IBM System/370 Model 168 computer complex.

Figure 5.5. IBM 4331 computer complex.

increased the main storage addressing capability by 128 times by extending the address field from 24 to 31 bits. At the same time, it maintained a 24-bit compatibility mode (upward compatibility), allowing application programs written for systems without this new option to run unchanged.

In February 1985, IBM extended the 30XX series with the addition of the IBM 3090 (Figure 5.6). This series, originally announced with the Models 200 and 400, extended the performance range of the System/370 architecture beyond that of the preceding members of the 30XX series. The 3090 series was later extended and became IBM's large-system flagship. The 370-XA added expanded storage to the 3090. Expanded storage was a new form of processor storage, separate from main storage, used to hold much more information inside the computer. This additional storage resulted in an overall system performance improvement.

The true test of any computer architecture is in the marketplace. Only by the life or death of the architecture do computer designers really know whether they have been successful. The longevity and extendibility of the System/360 and System/370 architectures speak highly of their original designers. In fact, Bob Evans, Fred Brooks, and Erich Block received the National Medal of Technology at a White House ceremony in 1985 for their part in developing the System/360.

Figure 5.6. IBM 3090 Model 200 computer complex.

The next advance in the architecture came in 1988 with the introduction of the Enterprise Systems Architecture/370 (ESA/370). This architecture again improved virtual storage addressing by enabling access to another form of virtual storage, called data spaces. Data spaces allow more data to reside in main and expanded storage, reducing input/output (I/O) and improving throughput. Other capabilities of the ESA/370 architecture made it easier for information to be shared among the users of the system.

In September 1990, IBM introduced the Enterprise System Architecture/390 (ESA/390) and the ES/9000 family of computers covering the range of price/performance previously held by the System/ 370 9370, 43XX, and 3090 computers. The ESA/390 architecture and the 18 original models of the ES/9000 line again maintained application program compatibility all the way back to the first System/ 360 computers while enhancing performance and increasing functionality. ESA/390 included many new features, such as ESCON and parallel sysplex, continuing IBM's evolution of its large business computer architecture.

In 1994, IBM announced extensions to the System/390 (S/390) family including additions to the ES/9000 line and introduced new, scalable System/390 parallel-processing computers in a parallel sysplex environment. For IBM, two new computing directions were set with this announcement. CMOS (Complementary Metal Oxide Semiconductor) technology was introduced as a building block for very large computers, complementing bipolar technology; and computers targeting specific application environments—rather than the full general-purpose environment—were introduced. Later announcements extended the CMOS technology to low-end, standalone servers and then to a broad range of servers providing performance not quite to the top of the older bipolar technology processors. These changes reduced the overall cost of computing for businesses while providing them with greater flexibility. Over time, new System/390 models were announced to replace the ES/9000 models, and the evolution of this long popular family continues.

IBM continued the evolution of the S/390 with the addition of the Generation 3 (G3), the Generation 4 (G4), Generation 5 (G5), and finally the Generation 6 (G6) Enterprise Server lines, each providing highly scalable processing power in a parallel sysplex environment. During these years, there was a major shift in the S/390 processing family. Gone were the days where the S/390 processor complex occupies floors of computing space. These newer systems were compact, air-cooled processors that occupied significantly less floor space and required a fraction of the energy that was required with the processors used earlier in the 1990s, while providing many times the processing power of their predecessors. Computer rooms that once were filled with IBM S/390 processing power now appear empty—not because the mainframe has been replaced, but simply because of the reduced space that the S/390 processing complex requires. The S/390 physically smaller processors have improved in processing power to the point where they can replace much-larger bipolar processors.

One thing that enabled these changes was the shift shift to new technology for its microprocessors which started in 1994. The new technology, known as Complementary Metal Oxide Semiconductors (CMOS), replaced the earlier technology, which was known as bipolar processors. A fundamental difference between the two technologies enabled a shift from a water-cooled processor requiring significant environmental investment to a simplified, air-cooled processor, requiring significantly reduced infrastructure. The improvements that CMOS made possible are nearly unbelievable. Whereas a state-of-the-art machine in the early 1990s weighed over 31,000 pounds, the G4 CMOS-based server weighs in at only 2,100 pounds. The number of parts required dropped from over 6,000 parts in the ES9000 to only 92 parts in the newer G4.

For the smaller environments, IBM also introduced the S/390 Multiprise 2000, and Multiprise 3000 systems that package both software and hardware into a single offering. These offerings are particularly interesting to software developers who are looking for lower cost platforms for S/390 software development.

Then in October of 2000, IBM introduced its next generation of server families under the IBM @server brand name. One of these new families was based on the S/390 family and called the @server zSeries. The first new zSeries server was the z900 positioned to replace the S/390 G5 and G6 processors. The remainder of this chapter focuses on the new @server zSeries systems and the most current S/390 environment.

The Basics of a zSeries or S/390 Computer System

The zSeries and S/390 systems provide a highly sophisticated computing environment. Figure 5.7 shows the basic elements that make up a bare-bones zSeries or S/390 computer system (suitable for testing a system but not for executing a productive workload). The processor unit houses the millions of electronic circuits that form the heart of the computer. Within the processor unit there are one or more central processors (CPs)—the elements that actually execute the computer programs. Systems that use a single CP are called uniprocessors. Those that utilize multiple central processors to achieve higher performance levels are called multiprocessor models. These are designed to operate as a single image (dyadic or triadic models for example) or to be physically partitionable into two separate processors.

Even when a single computer system employs multiple central processors, it appears to the system operator and users to be a single system (i.e., it presents a single-system image). However, any zSeries

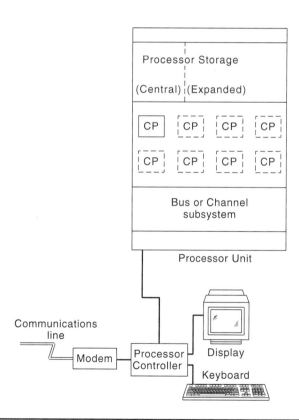

Figure 5.7. S/390 processor unit, power/coolant distribution unit, and processor controller.

or S/390 computer, regardless of the number of central processors, can be divided logically into parts so that it gives the appearance of multiple computers to the users and to the system operator. This is called logical partitioning, and it is facilitated by the Processor Resource/Systems Manager (PR/SM) logical partitioning. With PR/SM, a single computer can be divided into logical partitions (LPARs), each of which provides a somewhat isolated computing environment.

The processor storage (often called central storage or main memory) holds the programs and data upon which the central processor(s) acts. It is made up of two different regions of memory: central storage and expanded storage. Central storage is the traditional type of memory found in most computers, from the smallest personal computers to supercomputers. It is a high-speed storage area used to hold information currently needed by the processor unit. This information is addressed a single byte at a time.

Expanded storage, though still residing within the processor unit, is usually a little slower and less expensive to use than central storage. Expanded storage holds information beyond the immediately pertinent information being used in central storage. This information is addressed only in increments of 4,000 bytes (4 KB), referred to as a page. Staging information in expanded storage avoids the need to retrieve this information from even slower external storage devices (such as a disk drive). Thus, expanded storage provides a relatively low-cost method of increasing the amount of information held in the processor unit, typically resulting in an overall increase in the performance of the computer system.

A channel subsystem, available on all zSeries and S/390 computers, provides a standard way to attach optional devices such as networking peripherals or direct-storage devices to the computers. Although it is generally necessary to attach external devices in order to make a complete computer system, the choice of which peripherals to connect depends on the user's needs. Historically, the S/390 was connected to a communications network by using a specialized networking peripheral attached to the S/390 using the channel subsystem. But with the zSeries and newer S/390 processors, the Open Systems Adapter can be used as an alternative means of connecting the computer system to a communications network.

Also shown in Figure 5.7 is the processor controller. This device starts up, configures, and maintains the computer. It is the "cockpit" of the computer system and is used exclusively by the personnel who support the system, not by the business application users of the system. The processor controller consists of a small computer, a display, and a keyboard.

Attached to the processor controller is a modem. The modem enables the processor controller, if authorized, to send and receive information over a telephone line. This modem link allows the computer, for example, to automatically call an IBM remote support facility and electronically report any problems detected with the system.

Although the computer shown in Figure 5.7 could be set up and tested, it lacks devices required to perform useful work. Figure 5.8 adds the devices necessary to make a functional computer system. A Direct Access Storage Device (DASD) subsystem is added to provide disk storage for the system. Whereas the processor storage holds pro-

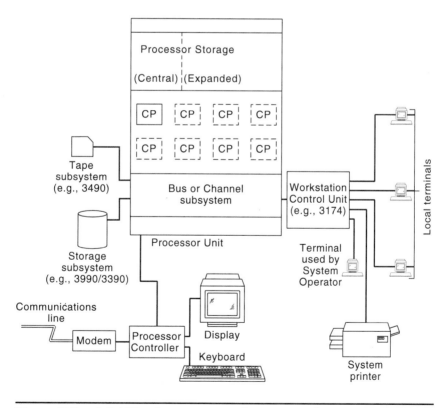

Figure 5.8. A DASD subsystem, tape subsystem, workstations, and printers must be attached to the S/390 to make a complete computer system.

grams and data currently being acted upon by the central processor(s), disk storage holds programs and data not currently being used but that may be needed at any instant.

A tape subsystem is used to store data that is less-frequently processed than data on disks (for example, large sequential files), to hold archival data, and to provide a level of backup in the event of system failure. Frequently, information stored on the DASDs is backed up to magnetic tape either to use DASD space more efficiently or to ensure a backup copy if the DASD should fail. The tape subsystem also provides a way to load program products (which often are distributed on tape) into the system and to exchange programs and data with other computer systems.

To allow people to interact with the computer, workstations are attached to it. A workstation is either a simple device with a display and keyboard, a network computer, or a complete computer system, such as a personal computer. With the growth of the Internet and the new breed of communications devices such as Personal Digital Assistants (PDAs), the devices which can access the computer system are now virtually unlimited.

Traditionally, communication between the workstation and the S/390 was performed using an IBM communications protocol known as Systems Network Architecture (SNA). With SNA, the workstations could be attached to a local workstation control unit, which manages the traffic flow between the workstations and either the channel subsystem (for local communications) or another networking device (for remote communications with the S/390). If this workstation control unit is directly attached to the channel subsystem of S/390 computers, it is called a local workstation control unit.

With the advent of intranet and Internet technologies, many people are replacing their SNA network access to the S/390 with TCP/IP network access. With TCP/IP access, the workstation will typically communicate with a router, or networking switch, that is part of the TCP/IP network. This router, or switch, typically connects to a network of other routers and switches that ultimately provide access to the computer itself. Capabilities now exist for both SNA-based and TCP-IP based application programs to operate on the same computer system, while utilizing an industry standard TCP/IP network.

With the introduction of the S/390 Generation 5, a new means of network connectivity for the S/390 was introduced which provides the highest speed access ever. OSA-Express is included as an alternative for connecting the S/390 to a communications network.

zSeries 900—The New Generation

In October of 2000, IBM introduced the IBM ~ zSeries 900—the first zSeries server. It is build on IBM's new z/Architecture which extends the S/390 architecture. The z/Architecture provides a new 64-bit symmetric multiprocessing (SMP) foundation. It allows for systems that can be partitioned (to act as if they were more than one computer) or clustered (combining the computing power of up to 640 processors) to meet fast changing demands of the emerging e-business world. Features such as the Intelligent Resource Director (IRD) which automatically reallocate processor and I/O resources (e.g. memory and disk storage) from one LPAR (logical partition) to another to help handle spikes in demand.

The zSeries 900 (also called the z900) is build using a new type of packaging module that can house up to 20 processors. Up to 16 of these processors can work together in a SMP environment with the remaining four used to help manage thinks like I/O processing or system recovery. Future systems will include HiperSockets which provide high speed pathways for Internet (TCP/IP) connections between separate operating systems running on the same system. These HiperSockets will improve the performance of e-business applications.

IBM also introduced new versions of popular operating systems to be used with the z900 systems including z/OS (based on OS/390), z/VM (based on VM), Linux for zSeries (a popular industry standard operating system). z/OS has features that help z900 systems react to unpredictable changes in demand through features like IRD and the Workload Manager (WLM) which lets you specify priorities within the system. For example, you can use Workload manager to specify that "90 percent of the requests coming in from a given URL (Web site address) should complete with 0.5 seconds." This allows you to align system capabilites with business goals. The z900 systems can also run the S/390 versions of these operating systems.

S/390 Multiprise Enterprise Servers

IBM also saw the need to offer an S/390 model for the smaller enterprise. The Multiprise 2000 Server was created to provide an upgrade path for smaller S/390 users while providing a reduced cost. The reduced overall cost was possible through the use of CMOS technology—which provides an internal disk, enables communications through the S/390 Open Systems Adapter/2 feature, and offers environmental efficiencies. The systems come with packaged solutions and the latest S/390 operating systems ready to use.

In 1999, IBM introduced the Multiprise 3000 Enterprise Server. The Multiprise 3000 Enterprise Server is a package of hardware and software. The software included is focused on allowing one to easily use the S/390 for several different business environments, including establishing e-business environments.

A Look Inside the zSeries and S/390

Many components and structures work together to make up a complete computer system. In this section, we will take a quick look inside zSeries and S/390.

Storage Hierarchy—Making Data Available

As defined earlier, central processors actually manipulate the data as necessary to do work for the user. The rest of the computer system basically feeds information (programs and data) to the central processor or accepts information from it. If the rest of the computer system cannot keep pace with the central processors, the system is constrained and overall system performance is reduced. Thus, the rest of the computer system must be carefully balanced with the central processor(s) for maximum efficiency. To achieve balanced performance in a cost-effective manner, most computer systems (including the zSeries and S/390) employ several types of information storage devices with varying performance levels. In other words, they have a storage hierarchy. (Figure 5.9 illustrates the storage hierarchy.)

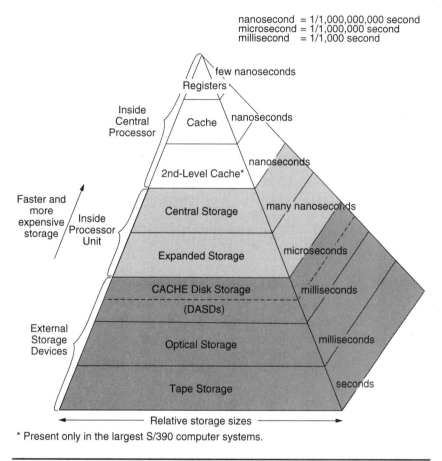

nanosecond = 1/1,000,000,000 second
microsecond = 1/1,000,000 second
millisecond = 1/1,000 second

few nanoseconds
Registers

Inside
Central
Processor

Cache   nanoseconds

nanoseconds

2nd-Level Cache*

Faster and
more
expensive
storage

Inside
Processor
Unit

Central Storage   many nanoseconds

Expanded Storage   microseconds

CACHE Disk Storage   milliseconds

(DASDs)

External
Storage
Devices

Optical Storage   milliseconds

Tape Storage   seconds

Relative storage sizes

* Present only in the largest S/390 computer systems.

Figure 5.9.   Storage hierarchy in S/390 computers.

The whole purpose of the storage hierarchy in computers is to respond as quickly as possible to the central processor's relentless requests for the retrieval and storage of information. To achieve this, the system constantly adjusts and moves information among the different levels of the storage hierarchy, placing the information most likely to be needed next as high in the hierarchy as possible.

The computer system's full performance potential is realized only when information is kept as high in the storage hierarchy as possible.

For this reason, each computer is configured (or tuned) to provide the correct amount of each storage type for the environment in which it is used—something not always easy to predict. As the environment changes, it may become necessary to expand various types of storage to keep the system running at its best.

Processor Storage

At the top of the storage pyramid are the registers, which are very fast circuits inside the central processor that hold only the programming instructions and data on which the execution units (also within the central processor) are acting. Since they are in the central processor and are extremely high-speed circuits (which switch in a few nanoseconds), they are very efficient at meeting the immediate storage needs of the central processor's execution units.

Next in the storage pyramid is the cache storage, an array of very high-speed electronic memory circuits that are also found in each central processor. The cache storage contains the next instruction to be fed to the central processor's execution units.

The second-level buffer, next in the storage pyramid, resides outside the central processor. It automatically collects information from the next pyramid layer (central storage) and stages that information for the cache. The whole purpose of the second- level buffer is to provide information to the cache more quickly than could be done by the central storage. Like the cache storage, the second-level buffer consists of an array of very high-speed electronic memory circuits.

Central storage, made up of a large array of high-speed electronic circuits that reside inside the processor unit, is the pivot point of the storage hierarchy. All information to be acted upon by any central processor or I/O channel must reside, at some point, in central storage. It is much larger than the pyramid layers above it, but it still provides information to the central processor(s) very quickly. Central storage is known also as memory, main storage, and Random Access Memory (RAM).

The next layer in the storage pyramid is expanded storage, a cost-effective way to augment central storage without sacrificing too much in performance. It consists of a very large array of electronic memory circuits that act as an overflow area for central storage. In some S/390 computers, expanded storage is a region of central storage that behaves like expanded storage. This allows those S/390 computers to comply with the requirement defined in the ESA/390 architecture to have expanded storage. In the larger S/390 computers, expanded storage actually is electronic circuits set apart from the central storage circuitry. Information that is still likely to be needed but cannot quite fit into central storage is moved automatically to expanded storage. All of the information stored in expanded storage, however, must be moved back to central storage before being accessed by the central processors. The S/390 computer hardware and operating system manage this information transfer, relieving the programmer from having to understand the different memory subsystems. In fact, the central processors do not know that expanded storage exists. Together, central storage and expanded storage are referred to as processor storage.

External Storage

The next layer in the storage pyramid is disk storage, provided by Direct Access Storage Devices (DASDs), which are subdivided into DASDs with a high-speed cache for performance and DASDs without cache. DASDs are the first type of storage covered so far that physically resides outside the processor unit. They exist as I/O devices attached through one or more I/O channels or system buses. DASDs are also the first storage covered so far that is able to retain information even when the power is turned off. Thus, disk storage is said to be permanent storage.

Issues related to external storage are no longer "peripheral." The speed with which organizations create new data and information, new applications that require a "data warehouse," the growing amounts of business-critical information on workstations, and the development of open-system architectures all drive changes to the way data is managed. Capacity is no longer the primary issue. Rather, data availability, performance of the access method, data security and integrity, and data-storage costs are driving rapid changes to computing environments. Nevertheless, the basic interactions between external storage and internal storage remain the same.

Like expanded storage, information stored on DASDs must be moved to central storage before it is available to a central processor. There is generally a delay (measured in millionths of a second) from the time the central processor requests the information until the time that it is available inside the central processor. This delay results from the fact that DASDs are electromechanical devices, which are slower than electrical devices because they are constrained by mechanical motion. Further, since the DASDs are located outside the processor unit, the information is brought in through an I/O operation, which involves additional subsystems (I/O channel or system bus and a control unit) and the delays associated with them. If, however, DASD with cache is used and the data is within the cache, the mechanical motion and the reading from disk are eliminated. Data is transferred directly from the cache in response to the I/O operation. With a write-through cache, a write operation does not need to wait for the data to be written to disk before freeing the channel. When the data reaches the cache, the channel is freed for other operations, and the write then occurs synchronously from cache to disk.

The next layer of the storage pyramid is optical storage. Information that is used infrequently or that traditionally has been stored on paper or microfiche can be stored cost-effectively using optical storage. Unlike DASDs and tape, which use magnetic recording technology to save information, optical storage uses light from a laser to write and read information on disks that are kept in a robotic library.

Finally, the lowest level of the storage pyramid is tape storage. Tape consists of a long, flexible strip coated with magnetic material and rolled onto a reel or into a cartridge. A tape drive reads and writes information on the tape much as a cassette recorder records and plays music on audiocassette tapes. The tape drive runs the tape across the read/write head. Early tapes had physical contact between the tape and the read/write head, but today's tape drives do not; the tape rides over the head on a cushion of air. Electrical impulses in the read/write head transfer information to and from the tape's surface. One primary purpose of tape storage is to provide a backup storage medium for information in the computer's disk storage. Tape is also commonly used in distributing programs and transferring information from one computer system to another. For general-purpose information archival and disk storage backup, tape is often used over optical storage due to its lower cost. Tape continues to be the frequently chosen medium for sequential processing applications because of its high data transfer rate.

Open Systems Adapters

The Open Systems Adapters provide an alternative to the S/390 channel for connecting the Parallel Enterprise Server to communications networks. The OSA Adapters have evolved from the OSA-1 and OSA-2 adapters which while providing network connectivity to the S/390, did not match the performance of the S/390 channel connectivity. However with the introduction of OSA Express on the Generation 5 processors, networks can now be connected to the S/390 using industry standard connectivity, but with the highest throughput ever before possible.

Parallel Sysplex

A parallel sysplex is a group of two or more zSeries or S/390 computer systems operating as one computer system. The purpose of a parallel sysplex is to allow users to combine the processing power of more than one system while having them appear (to the system operators and users) to be one large computer system—called a single-system image. It enables them to cooperate as a single, logical computing facility by synchronizing their time references and enabling them to share data at the record level while preserving data integrity. While doing this, it keeps its underlying structure transparent to users, networks, applications, and operations management. Benefits of a parallel sysplex include synergy with existing applications, continuous availability, single-image operations, dynamic workload balancing, and data sharing and integrity across multiple processors.

In a single system, growth is limited by the size of the system. Managing the system, however, is relatively easy because all of the resources are under the control of one copy of the operating system. Taking a large workload application (such as transaction processing) and permitting it to run on a large number of separate systems adds capacity for growth but significantly complicates managing the workload, which includes distributing the workload effectively across all of the systems. The parallel sysplex solves this problem by providing the flexibility of multiple systems with the simplicity of a single-system image. Transaction-processing workloads are dynamically balanced across processors, and, with the introduction of high-performance coupling technology, data is also dynamically shared at a fine level of granularity with read and write access and full data integrity (Figure 5.10). The shared data model simplifies planning for new business applications; dynamic workload balancing manages changing patterns of use; and the parallel sysplex participates as an element of an open, network computing environment.

Coupling Facility

The Coupling Facility makes high-performance, multisystem data sharing possible. It provides high-speed locking, caching, and message list services between zSeries or S/390 processors that are connected by coupling links to the coupling facility in a parallel sysplex. To ensure fault tolerance and high-availability redundant characteristics for a production environment, more than one coupling facility is required.

There are multiple choices for providing the parallel sysplex coupling facility support. One choice is for the standalone coupling facil-

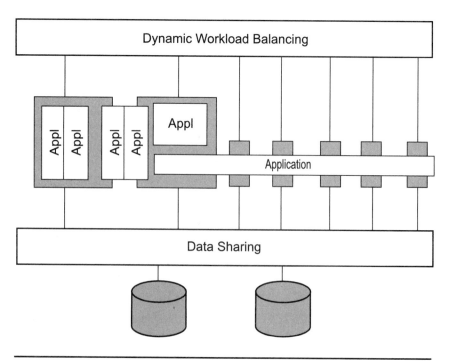

Figure 5.10. Interrelationship of parallel sysplex features.

ity to be based on the CMOS technology used in the parallel enterprise server. The standalone support is provided by a separate, independent processor within the sysplex. A second option is to execute
the Coupling Facility Control Code (CFCC) in a logical partition
(LPAR) of the 9672 server. Finally, an Integrated Coupling Migration Facility (ICMF) on an ES/9000 711- or 511-based processor or a
9672 parallel server can be used for the coupling facility support. A
third choice is to use one of the "spare processors" within the system
to perform the Coupling Facility function. The choice of which method
to use involves numerous tradeoffs between cost and availability.

zSeries and S/390 Software

Although the system hardware is a critical element of the computing
environment, so is the software. The software provides the operating
environment, utilities, and application logic to perform a given task on
the selected computing hardware. zSeries and S/390 software is unique
in its ability to handle tens of thousands of users simultaneously.

Types of Software—A Model

The software used in zSeries and S/390 computers is depicted in the
simple software model shown in Figure 5.11. Three basic categories
(or software layers) of software are used with S/390 computers: application program, operating system, and Licensed Internal Code
(LIC). Each software layer performs a completely different job, but
all three interoperate to perform useful work for the users.

Application Programs

The top software layer in the software model is the application program layer (the top layer in Figure 5.11). Application programs perform the tasks (Web serving or database management for example)
for which the computer was purchased, but the other two layers play
essential support roles. The "User's View" arrows in the figure indicate that the user interacts most often with an application program

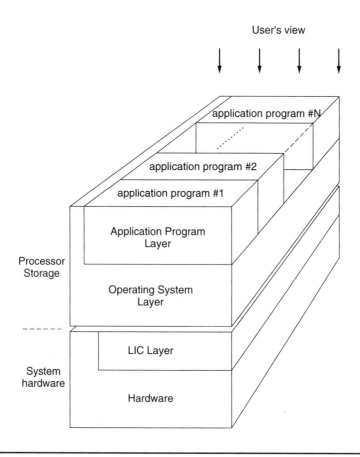

Figure 5.11. Software model of System/390's basic software structure.

and less frequently with the operating system. Working closely with the other software layers, the application program processes the various keystrokes made by the user and responds by displaying information on the computer's display or other output devices.

In general, programs written for earlier computers in the family (e.g. S/370 or S/390) to be executed directly on zSeries computers. This compatibility allows users to bring forward their investment in application program development, database design, and user training when upgrading their hardware. Frequently, application programs in the business environment are used for such tasks as e-business Web site serving, accounting, financial modeling, database management, electronic mail (e-mail), and computer graphics. Application programs interact directly with the operating system to perform different tasks (such as reading and writing disk storage or sending information over a communications network). The interaction between the operating system and application programs takes place through the Application Programming Interface (API) presented by the operating system. Program products, called application enablers, extend the API presented by the operating system. Application enablers add function to the API, thus offering more services to application programs (Figure 5.12). As the figure shows, application enablers reside between the

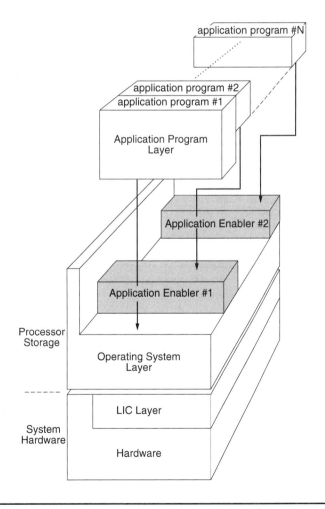

Figure 5.12. Application enablers build on the API of the operating system, offering additional services to application programs.

operating system and the application program layers of our software model, and they actively communicate with both layers.

By adding services to the API, application enablers make the job of application program development easier. This enables software-development companies to develop prewritten application programs more easily, providing users with more prewritten application programs from which to choose. In the same way, the productivity of developing custom application programs is improved, since the application enablers provide many functions that the developer would otherwise have to write from scratch during the custom application development project. IBM's DB2 is an example of a database application enabler family of products. IBM's CICS products are examples of transaction-processing application enablers. IBM's WebSphere products are examples of Web-enablement applications.

Operating System

The next layer in our software model is the operating system. The operating system manages the hardware resources of the computer system and performs tasks under the control of application programs and keyboard commands typed by the users. Because the application program can rely on the operating system to perform many of the detailed housekeeping tasks associated with the internal workings of the computer, the operating system is said to provide the operating system environment in which application programs execute. Since the application program interacts directly with the operating system, application programs are generally designed to work under a specific operating system. Operating systems also accept commands directly from the users to copy files, change passwords, and perform various other tasks.

LIC

The third and final layer of software in our model is the Licensed Internal Code (LIC). LIC is a set of highly specialized programs written by the manufacturer of a computer and rarely modified by either system operators or users. The set of LIC in zSeries and S/390 computers is embedded deeply within the computer system and is therefore considered to be part of the computing machine itself rather than part of a program running on the machine. Unlike application programs or the operating system, only other programs use LIC; that is, LIC never interacts directly with the user or the programmer. LIC exists only to help the hardware perform the more-complex instructions in the architecture. The LIC includes the programming executed by the many different microprocessors in a computer. For example, some LIC is executed by the microprocessors used to implement the I/O channels.

The LIC approach helps shield the hardware details of the processor unit from the software's view of the processor unit. That is, it preserves compliance with architecture, and thus compatibility with operating systems and application programs, in the face of evolutionary hardware improvements.

When data is sent to a computer from an external source, such as a workstation, the software layers of our model come into play. First, the I/O channels and associated LIC verify that all went well in receiving the data; then the LIC notifies the operating system that the data is correct, ready, and waiting for use. The operating system makes the data available to the application program and then reactivates the application program, which was dormant waiting for the next keystroke(s). The application program processes the data as necessary and instructs the operating system to wait for the next keystrokes, and the whole cycle starts all over again.

Computers easily perform these steps in small fractions of a second. Similar but more complicated cooperation among the three software layers occurs for most functions performed by the computer, such as reading or writing a file on a DASD and communicating with other computers.

Operating Systems

Operating systems help manage the internal workings of a computer system and provide services to users and other programs. zSeries and S/390 computers can use one of several different operating systems. Next, we briefly examine some of these operating systems.

z/OS and OS/390

IBM's new z/OS is the latest evolution of the popular OS/390 operating system used on S/390 computers. Both z/OS and OS/390 provides a robust, mission-critical operating system. They represent a broad base of functionality, probably richer than any other computing environment. They allow S/390 systems to run traditional S/390 applications, UNIX applications, and object-oriented applications—even applications developed using Java technologies.

Both operating systems provide a powerful integrated WebSphere application server for the e-business environment and include integrated communications functions through the SecureWay Communications Server. This provides SNA and significantly improved TCP/IP communications protocols and industry-leading security through its security server functions.

Both OS/390 and z/OS provide support for the parallel sysplex environment for both SNA and TCP environments through exploitation of the Work Load Manager (WLM) function, which enables computing tasks within the computer system to be balanced across the multiple processors within the same computer system.

The z/OS operating system is the next generation operating system designed to take advantage of the new 64-bit z/Architecture introduced with the @server zSeries 900 systems. It includes other enhancements like the Intelligent Resource Director (IRD) which automatically reallocate processor and I/O resources (e.g. memory and disk storage) from one LPAR (logical partition) to another to help handle spikes in demand.

z/VM and VM

The virtual machine, or VM, operating system gets its name from the fact that it uses the virtual-storage concept to subdivide a single computer system into multiple, virtual computer systems, each with its own processor storage, disk storage, tape storage, and other I/O devices. That is, VM uses software techniques to make a single computer appear to be multiple computer systems. Each of these simulated computers (called virtual machines) acts as an independent and complete computer system. In some cases, a virtual machine is like an S/390-compatible "personal computer" with a single-user operating system serving the needs of a single user (or application program). A group of single-user virtual machines can be linked together to create a virtual local area network of computers within a single system all simulated by software (Figure 5.13).

Alternatively, a single virtual machine can run a multiuser operating system (for example, z/OS) and serve the needs of many users. VM's unique approach to resource management (that is, subdividing a single computer system into multiple, virtual computer systems, each with its own resources) makes it especially useful for interactive

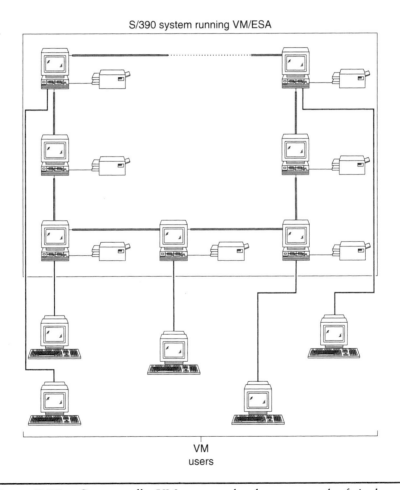

Figure 5.13. Conceptually, VM creates a local area network of single-user computers within an S/390 system.

computing, client/server computing, and running multiple operating systems. Interactive computing provides for flexible dialog between users and application programs, allowing users to perform ad hoc queries to databases, to write memos, or to perform mechanical design. Today, VM's large-scale interactive computing capabilities include support for thousands of office users, data analysis and decision support, advanced database processing, application development, and ad hoc problem solving.

VM provides a powerful function that enables other operating systems to run using VM as the underlying operating system. These other operating systems running under VM in a virtual machine are called guest operating systems. The efficiencies generated through VM's acting as a "host" system, in which resources are shared among multiple different systems on a single processor, make it practical to use VM to create, test, and run applications from any zSeries or S/390 operating environment. This simplifies migration and experimentation with new platforms and functions. zSeries systems can run either VM/ESA or the z/VM version written specially for the new zSeries systems.

VSE

The virtual storage extended, or VSE, operating system is used primarily in small to midsize S/390 computers. VSE/ESA is the descendant of the Disk Operating System (DOS) introduced in 1965 for use with the smaller models of the System/360 mainframe computer family. While there is no special version of VSE for zSeries systems, VSE/ESA is supported on zSeries systems.

The next evolutionary step after DOS was the Disk Operating System/Virtual Storage (DOS/VS) operating system, introduced in 1972. A major enhancement made in DOS/VS was the introduction of virtual storage—a feature of the operating system that makes a computer system seem to have more central storage than it actually has.

The next evolutionary step after DOS/VS came in 1983 with the introduction of Virtual Storage Expanded/System Package (VSE/SP). Even though the letters "DOS" were dropped from the name, VSE/SP was an enhanced version of DOS/VSE. Figure 5.14 shows how VSE/SP (Version 3.2) handled System/370 central storage. The Virtual Addressability Extensions (VAE) feature introduced with VSE/

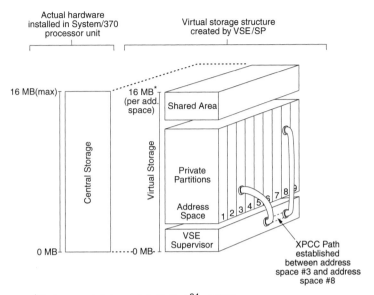

Figure 5.14. VSE/SP created multiple virtual address spaces.

SP allowed users to define multiple virtual address spaces, each identical to the single 16 MB virtual address space provided by DOS/VSE (Figure 5.15). Having multiple address spaces provides a much-needed expansion of central storage without losing compatibility with existing application programs.

Linux

Linux is a popular and fast-growing open-source (meaning anyone can customize it) operating system. It is available for many different computer systems including System/390. IBM has just released a new

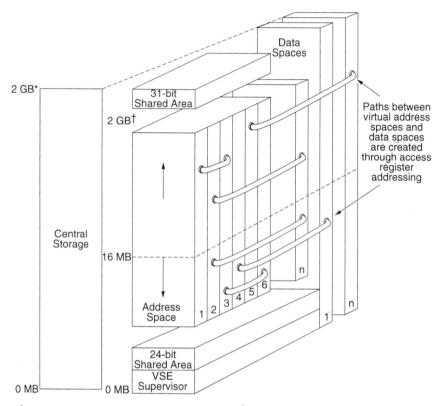

*Maximum central storage is architecturally limited to 2 GB. VSE/ESA design limit is 2 GB; but central storage supported is the lesser of processor central storage or 2 GB.

†Maximum virtual address range for an address space or a data space.

Figure 5.15. VSE/ESA Version 1, Release 3 supports 31-bit addressing and ESA/390 data spaces.

version called Linux for zSeries which is written to take advantage of the 64-bit z/Architecture.

By providing the Linux operating system on zSeries and S/390 systems, users are able to choose from hundreds of packages and tools developed by the large community of Linux developers.

6

Computer Communications

What good is a computer if it cannot communicate? The simple answer is "not much." In this chapter, we examine the underlying concepts behind several computer communications environments.

The Need to Communicate—An Introduction

If any one activity is most crucial to a business, it is the act of communicating information to the proper decision-maker. Based on the information available to that decision-maker, important choices are made that can have far-reaching effects on the success of the business. Improve communications in a business, and you are likely to improve productivity and profitability. Ironically, as a business grows, it becomes both more important yet more difficult to maintain efficient, accurate communications—the very thing that facilitates business growth in the first place. Communications difficulties grow exponentially with the size of the business.

Computers are a requirement in the business environment, and with few exceptions, computers must have the ability to communicate. This communication can occur directly between two computers. However, more typically, it occurs among a group of computers in a communications network allowing business information to move at electronic speeds. Communications may occur locally, or between geographically dispersed computers, allowing users at remote locations access to vital business information.

With the growth of the Internet (discussed in Chapter 1), communications is no longer an option—it is a requirement. Immediate communication is a necessity both between computers and between millions of end users and thousands of computing systems. With the Internet, a customer may visit a single Web site, which then interfaces to numerous computer systems. For example, planning for a simple business trip might require communications with an airline reservation system, a car rental reservation system, a hotel reservation system, a weather service, and more. Obviously, this is not possible without effective communication.

Traditional computer communications required some type of physical connection between the computers, whether it was a local area network provided within the enterprise or a wide area network provided by the telephone company. But with the rapid emergence of new technologies, communications between computers may even occur over wireless connections, requiring no physical connection media between the computers. All of IBM's computer families are designed to participate in a wide range of communications environments.

The Internet

There is no question that the Internet has changed how we communicate more than any invention since the printing press. Communication between computers connected to the Internet occurs using a "language" know as the TCP/IP communications protocol. The beauty of the Internet is that most of us are totally unaware of TCP/IP, or any of the underlying details of the communications protocols that we utilize. We access the Internet through an Internet Service Provider (ISP), or connect through our company's Local Area Network (LAN). In either case, when we use the latest advances in TCP/IP technology, communication appears simple.

But is communication that simple? Not at all! The Internet is extremely sophisticated, consisting of multiple interconnected communications networks, each consisting of thousands of devices called routers and switches that take the data that you wish to communicate and forward the information toward your intended destination. Each of these devices works in cooperation to ensure that the computers accomplish their intended communication.

Although the Internet provides a means for computers to communicate, it actually provides just the plumbing for the connection. Think of it much like the telephone. The telephone provides the medium over which two people can communicate. But what happens when two people who speak different languages try to talk each other? Can they communicate? Probably not, unless they determine a common language that they will use. The same is true for computer communications. The computers must share a common language, whether it be a File Transfer Protocol (FTP) to exchange a file, Web Server access provided by browsers such as Netscape Navigator and Microsoft Internet Explorer, or some other protocol specific to the application used by the two communicating computers.

Many schemes exist for connecting the Internet to traditional business data. A key point in each of these methods is that the business application does not have to be rewritten to provide access to its data from the Internet.

Intranets

Many internal communications networks within today's corporations are referred to as intranets. This name indicates that the network is based on Internet technology, but intranets often consist of multiple communications protocols. For example, typical intranets with on mainframes will support both SNA and TCP/IP protocols since traditional mainframe applications were predominantly built around the SNA communications protocol. However, with the continuing evolution of the TCP/IP protocol (whereby the protocol now has many of the characteristics of SNA) most corporations are moving toward TCP/IP or, more specifically, IP for their network transport. Data Link Switch (DLSw) and IBM's Enterprise Extender are two technologies that allow SNA applications to operate transparently over an IP network, enabling a single networking protocol within the corporate intranet.

Most corporations are struggling with providing what previously was "internal data" over the Internet to their business partners or customers. It is impractical to rewrite existing applications in order to make the data accessible across the Internet. Solutions are available through products such as IBM's WebSphere , CICS, and the recently announced Host Publisher product. Each of these offerings enable existing applications to be accessible over the Internet generally with minimal to no change to the existing application.

IBM introduced technology known as transcoding that has potential to revolutionize the reach of enterprise data. Transcoding allows data to be repurposed to new devices such as wireless phones and personal digital assistants, without the need to make any changes to the application programs themselves. "Legacy data" such as that provided by SNA applications, and Web data such as that provided by today's Web applications can be transcoded, or transformed, to meet the capabilities of the device, the preferences of the user, or the user's environment.

Network Types

Today's computer networks typically are very complex. They consist of a combination of locally connected computers that communicate with computers in different locations. The connection between the computers may consist of a physical wire, or it may have no physical connection at all. Next, we examine some of the different network types.

Local Area Networks

Just as there is a need for office personnel at any one location to talk frequently with each other, there is value to allowing the computers at a given location to communicate with each other efficiently and easily. Local area networks are a means of connecting computer systems together for the purposes of communication. LANs enable communications between a group of local computers that might be found in a department, building, or campus. Each computer attached to the LAN can share information, programs, and computer equipment such as printers with other computers in the network. The most common types of LANs include Ethernet and Token-Ring Network.

Wide Area Networks

When the need to share information and programs spans long distances such as between different branches of a bank, wide area networks (WANs) are used. WANs connect computer systems together across town or around the globe. WANs can be public networks like the Internet or private networks maintained by businesses, telephone companies, or other institutions. WANs can be built using various communications standards and protocols. Local area networks at different locations can communicate with each other by interconnecting using a WAN.

WANs consist of many differing technologies. Examples of the underlying technologies include frame relay and Asynchronous Transfer Mode (ATM). Typically, the higher-level networking protocol such as SNA or TCP/IP is unaware of the underlying transport technology.

Wireless Networks

Wireless networks consist of a variety of types. They may consist of a simple office network communicating via wireless technology (e.g. Bluetooth discussed in Chapter 1), computers connected directly using radio waves, or users connecting to an application over the Internet while using their wireless phone, or Personal Digital Assistant (PDA).

Wireless technology has improved substantially over the last few years. Early wireless connectivity was low speed and error prone. Today's wireless technologies are very reliable, and can support high-speed communications approaching speeds provided by early generation Local Area Networks.

Client Server Networking

In a service business, such as law or accounting, a "client" is someone who requests assistance from a specialized service provider. Lawyers provide legal services to their clients; they do not provide accounting services. Mechanics fix your car; they do not wash your windows. When you request help from a service provider, you find the right kind of provider, or "server," to meet your needs. Often, providers have knowledge you lack or can perform tasks more efficiently because they specialize. However, when you tell your accountant or your mechanic what you need done, you must understand at least a little of what they can do. Otherwise, they may not understand your needs properly.

Computing is no different. The key idea is this: The terms client and server refer to *software,* not to hardware. A software client is a computer program that doesn't know how to do everything. It therefore requests help from other software, the server software. Server software performs specific, specialized tasks effectively. A software server that understands printing probably would not be able to help a client that needs help retrieving a stock quote. Software clients are also like service business clients because software clients must interact with servers using a common language.

The Internet's popular World Wide Web is an example of client/server computing. The client is the Web browser program, and the server is the Web server that provides you with the Web pages you see. There are many other examples and implementations of client/server computing.

What Makes Up a Client/Server Computing System?

Figure 6.1 shows how the parts of a software client and a server relate. A software client usually consists of two pieces. The first piece is the client application software; the second is what we can call "client-enabling software." These two parts talk using a carefully specified common language, called an Application Programming Interface (API). Because computer programs must be specified precisely, the API determines exactly what interactions are possible between the client application software and the rest of the client/server system.

The client-enabling software takes any request the client application software makes via the API and verifies it for correctness. It then decodes the request and forwards it to one or more servers for action. Usually, the servers reside somewhere else on a network, so the client-enabling software also creates "links" or "sessions" over the

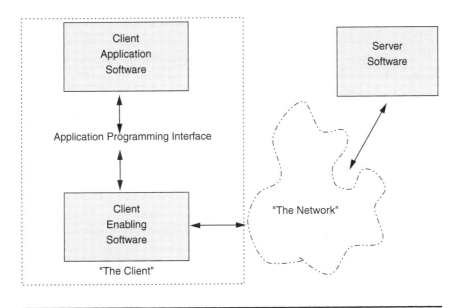

Figure 6.1. Client/server concept.

network to the servers. When the servers are finished, they send the results back to the client-enabling software. The client-enabling software then interprets these results and gives them back to the client application software via the API.

The complexity of the software typically can be divided at many points between the client and the server. It is possible in many cases to have most of the computing performed at the client, or, for the same computing problem, perhaps most of the processing occurs at the server. A client that requires minimal software as part of the client/server operation is called a thin client. Network computers are a special type of thin client that require that all their software be delivered over the network when needed. The same idea can be used for traditional thick (i.e. a full blown personal computer) clients to reduce the costs of maintaining today's client computer systems. Thick clients typically contain pre-installed software permitting local operation of the client without a requirement to communicate with a server.

Client-enabling software and server software generally talk using a binary language. (In other words, a language made up of only zeros and ones.) Humans find reading binary language difficult, but computers interpret it efficiently. A network carries the interactions between client-enabling software and the servers. The server software can usually accept requests from dozens, hundreds, or even tens of thousands of clients concurrently, dependent on the type of server being used. Clients may request services from one server or from many servers, depending on the application's needs.

Client/server computing environments usually encompass personal computers working hand in hand with larger, shared computers. The larger machines may store and retrieve shared data, provide large memories and greater processing power, or provide shared access to costly or specialized I/O devices. Using larger machines can also reduce operational costs.

Users of client/server computing software might work within the same building, using a LAN to communicate, or they might use client/server software using a WAN that links computer systems across global distances. Client/server computing can take place within an organization or between organizational or enterprise boundaries to support a business process.

Architectures for Client/Server Applications

An applications architecture is a blueprint used to build or buy applications software for use in business. Such an architecture defines the relationships between the various functions within the applications. It can also specify relationships between applications, and it can define how the applications software will relate to specific business functions. Below are a few observations specific to client/server computing.

Two-Tiered Client/Server Applications

A two-tiered applications architecture is the easiest way to design a client/server application. Someone defines the processing to be done and then decides if each work item is best done on the server or the client. For example, a business application might include several services, such as user interface, data access, transaction management, security, or communications. A firm might buy or build services such as these to include in an application. Most often, companies buy packages that provide these services. A company wants the rules and policies that run their business to be different from other firms, however. That is where their business provides unique value for customers.

It is easy to imagine allocating each needed service to a client or a server system. Depending upon the staff's sophistication and the demands the software puts on the hardware and the network, components are assigned where they fit best. This applications architecture is shown in Figure 6.2.

Many client/server computing products today fit this applications architecture. In a typical resource-sharing model workgroup, for example, members share hardware and data without regard to the way the business itself runs. The business rules may reside in the client application, or may remain on the server.

However, if software is built and used that defines and automates "methods of business," where do you put those rules? For example, say you decide to place them on the client and you want to change your accounts receivable practices: Instead of providing 15-day terms, you want to use 5-day terms with electronic payments. If you put the logic for this business rule on the client, you have to change the software on all your clients when you want to change policy. This will be much more difficult than changing business rules on a few server systems.

On the other hand, placing the data and logic that embody the rules on the server can intertwine them with other services, such as

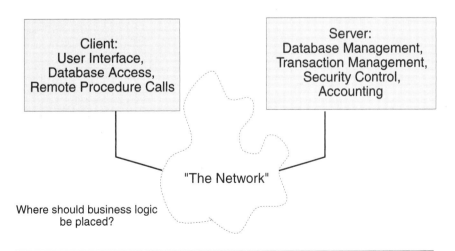

Figure 6.2. A sample two-tiered architecture.

transaction management and data access. This may make it harder for an organization to respond flexibly to local needs. If the business logic intertwines with other services, the application could become nearly monolithic, with all the rigidity this implies. Then, client/server computing would become a more-complex version of existing programs on shared systems.

Three-Tiered Client/Server Applications

Unlike two-tiered designs, the three-tiered approach directly recognizes the importance of your rules of business. It defines three layers: the user interface layer, the business logic layer (sometimes called the functional layer), and the data-access layer. In this view of building applications, all other services or components, such as a transaction manager or communications services, exist to make these three main components more effective. In building three tier applications, the three main components stay separate, even though two of them may eventually run on a single-server machine. Figure 6.3 shows this approach.

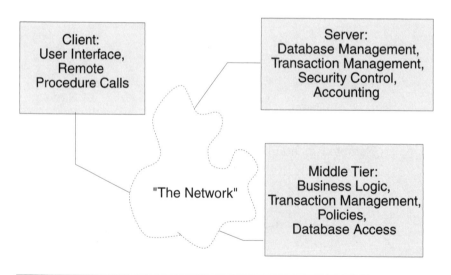

Figure 6.3. A sample three-tiered architecture.

7

IBM Global Services

Every business strives to improve profit while better serving its customers. The combination of information and Internet technologies that is creating the rapidly emerging e-business economy has become a powerful tool for reaching these twin goals. But properly planning, designing, implementing, and operating computer and Web-based solutions that deliver competitive advantage can be an incredibly complex task. That is why the demand for service providers with the skills and experience to help build and manage successful e-business and IT solutions is at an all time high.

Trends in the IT Services Marketplace

Services is the largest segment of the IT industry after software. Services is also the fastest growing segment. IDC, the industry research firm, forecasts that the market for IT services will grow 32 percent by 2003, to more than $470 billion. Services is also the leading driver of e-business investment. Worldwide, e-business spending is growing 19 percent per year, almost twice the rate of the IT industry overall; services accounts for over half of this market.

What is driving the growth in IT services? First, businesses are interlinking their business and IT strategies to achieve strategic *value creation.* Non-IT business executives are increasingly influencing IT decisions, and CIOs are more involved in strategic decision-making as IT moves from the role of a support function to being a business enabler.

The second driver of growth in IT services is the *complexity of technology.* The worldwide shortage of skills is driving businesses to service providers for their expertise in transforming IT into a competitive advantage. These factors are driving spending on integrated packaged solutions, strategic outsourcing, and out-tasking (also known as selective outsourcing).

Finally, *Internet technologies* are a major growth driver as the new e-business economy continues to expand dramatically. Businesses are increasingly migrating to connect the enterprise and its employees via intranets. They are also extending the value chain for business-to-business transactions by allowing customers, suppliers, and business partners to access data and applications through extranets—as well as to expand the business-to-consumer market through the global reach of the public Internet.

IBM Global Services Today

Today's economy is forcing businesses worldwide to address the challenges of globalization, advancing technologies, escalating competition and, most important, the e-business revolution. In this environment, companies increasingly demand comprehensive information technology services—not just software or hardware components—that will help them reduce costs, improve productivity, and maintain competitive advantage.

IBM Global Services is the world's largest business and technology services provider, with 1999 revenues of more than $32 billion. It is the fastest growing part of IBM, with more than 138,000 professionals serving businesses in 160 countries. Since 1991, IBM Global Services has been helping companies of all sizes manage their IT operations and resources, and ensure that their technology investments contribute to profitable growth.

IBM Global Services also has developed the industry's broadest array of e-business services, ranging from strategy consulting and Web integration to infrastructure services and Web hosting. IBM has over 15,000 e-business consultants who can draw on experience gained from more than 20,000 customer engagements worldwide as well as IBM's own transformation into what *BusinessWeek* has described as "...the largest dot.com of them all."

By leveraging the extensive research and technology resources of IBM, Global Services is well-positioned to lead businesses toward the new frontiers of e-business. In e-commerce, for instance, IBM research has generated more than 40 patents for e-market technologies. IBM also has developed technologies, software and services to capitalize on the coming wave of wireless e-business. By 2003, more people around the world will connect to the Web via wireless devices than by personal computers, according to the Yankee Group. IBM has developed a range of offerings, from Mobile e-business Consulting to Mobile Hosting and Operational Services.

Competitive Environment

IBM Global Services faces seven types of competitors: full service providers; consultants and systems integrators; local and niche providers; network, application and Internet service providers (ISPs); emerging e-business competitors; IT systems vendors; and value nets and partnerships.

The full services providers like EDS and Computer Sciences Corporation (CSC), are expanding aggressively. EDS has weathered major senior executive changes and is now focused on reducing costs and penetrating the exploding e-business market. It has created an e-business Solutions division to consolidate seven existing Web groups and 20,000 employees worldwide. CSC gets the largest part of its revenue—around 42 percent—from outsourcing, and is expected to increase that share.

Consultants and systems integrators such as Andersen Consulting have been IBM's fastest growing competitors, ranging from 25 percent a year growth up to 50 percent.

Andersen has been increasing their higher value offerings, such as strategy consulting and business process outsourcing. IBM's strategy to beat the Andersens of the world is to deliver e-business offerings, supply chain management (SCM), and customer relationship management (CRM), as well as establishing senior client executive relationships.

Local and niche providers either dominate a geography or have very targeted offerings. NTT, Japan's largest information services company, designs, assembles, leases and operates data links for major nationwide computer network users. SABRE is IBM's largest and most capable competitor in the travel and transportation solutions and services markets, operating what may be the world's largest electronic utility. To respond to these competitors, IBM is supplementing their strategic outsourcing with hosted business applications capabilities, focused business-based offerings, and e-business services with business process management (BPM). Network, application, and Internet service providers are becoming sought after business partners, growing quickly, and are often linking with e-business vendors. Exodus Communications is a provider of complex colocation Internet hosting services and network management solutions for businesses with mission-critical Internet operations. The company deploys and operates Internet Data Centers (IDCs) that function as virtual extensions of the businesses that colocate their Internet hardware servers, routers, and switches within Exodus' IDCs.

IT systems vendors, IBM's traditional competitors, are finding the value in services and joining the party, even if a little late. Hewlett Packard (HP) is developing outsourcing, financing, and integration services businesses, with emphasis on delivering these solutions under the tagline "e-services." Since these competitors generate most of their revenue from maintenance-based services, IBM's strategy is to drive their Total Systems Management (TSM) and extensive support services, such as systems management and business recovery.

Value nets and partnerships are not a new form of competition to IBM. They have competed many times when ad hoc alliances are formed to compete on megadeals. What is new, however, is that companies are now creating networks of services providers to recommend their software and hardware, in effect creating a full-service team.

Despite the fact that the range of competitors IBM Global Services faces every day is daunting—IBM has the skills, the offerings, and the strategy to maintain its leadership position.

IBM Global Service Offerings

IBM Global Services has organized its portfolio into three principal lines of business: Business Innovation Services, Integrated Technology Services, and Strategic Outsourcing Services. A fourth line of business called Learning Services supports the entire organization by delivering IT education and training services to businesses. Figure 7.1 shows how these offerings are organized. Now let's look at these four business areas.

Business Innovation Services

Speed is king in the e-business economy. New initiatives must go from cradle to launch in weeks, not months. At the same time, companies must do the hard work of integrating e-business into their existing processes and systems if they are to achieve lasting competitive advantage.

Business Innovation Services delivers the integrated e-business solutions businesses need to compete in the Internet economy. With expertise across 21 industries, IBM's e-business consultants help companies capitalize on new business models, align IT initiatives with business objectives, and create management systems that keep Web initiatives on track and generating solid returns.

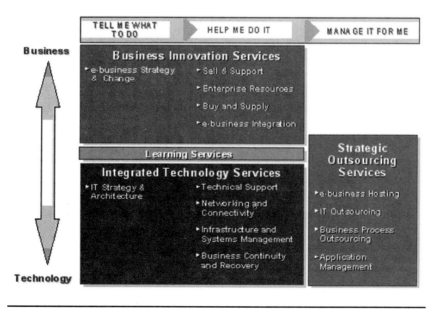

Figure 7.1. IBM Global Services portfolio and lines of business.

In 1999, IBM Global Services launched the Centers for IBM e-business Innovation, a global network of design and development laboratories. The centers bring together e-business strategists, marketing specialists, interactive designers, Web application developers, and systems integration specialists—all the necessary resources to help companies move to the next generation of e-business. The centers showcase the full spectrum of e-business services available from IBM Global Services and its business partners.

Through Business Innovation Services, IBM can quickly deploy multidisciplinary project teams that target the areas businesses consider most important to growth. Now let's look at some example services in the five solution catagories.

e-business Strategy and Change

In this category, IBM's consultants help you formulate a strategic business design that is customer relevant and profitable in the new networked economy. They work with a business to identify and analyze market opportunities and to anticipate competitive behavior. Then IBM helps the business define and prioritize potential ebusiness initiatives and create the architecture, business processes and operational model to pilot and deploy them.

Sell and Support

This category addresses customer needs to lower sales and marketing costs, extend market reach using new channels, and improve responsiveness and service quality. e-commerce Services is a family of offerings designed to assist businesses in preparing and conducting secure Internet business transactions both with other businesses and with their customers. Services range from assessments and strategy workshops, to the planning and implementation of specific business solutions. With Interactive Branding and Design Services, IBM helps a business establish, define, and transition a business' traditional brand into a customer experience in the online market space by understanding a business' organizations goals, objectives, market position, and target audience. We then develop unique solutions, maintaining a business' key attributes and value propositions, that build brand equity online.

With Customer Relationship Management Services, IBM provides consulting and systems integration/customization services to deliver e-business solutions around leading Customer Relationship Management packages. IBM utilizes standard methodologies that allow businesses to identify, select, acquire, develop, and retain profitable customers.

Business Intelligence Services involve the definition, development, and deployment of data centric applications that are focused on improved decision making capabilities. Key Business Intelligence services include data warehouse development, design and planning, strategy, decision optimization, solution delivery, process outsourcing, infrastructure proof of concept, application proof of concept, data quality improvement, data warehouse technology enablement, balanced scorecard deployment, and systems integration method. In addition, industry specific services are available for retailers, insurance, and telecommunications.

With Web-Selling Services, IBM builds interactive, e-business applications using best-of-breed technologies while leveraging a business' data and existing IT investment. IBM has developed a library of technology assets that enable rapid development of e-business solutions intended to get their customer to market faster.

Enterprise Resources

This category addresses customer needs internal to the enterprise that are transaction oriented around production, delivery and accounting processes.

With Enterprise Application Services, IBM helps apply best business practices and integrate core business processes with standard applications like SAP, Baan, Oracle, PeopleSoft, and J. D. Edwards to offer a total, cohesive suite of consulting and implementation services covering: strategy, industry and business consulting package selection, customization and integration, organization, change management, education and training, IT infrastructure consulting, application management, and outsourcing.

Many companies are considering extensions to their Enterprise Resource Planning (ERP) solutions to help them drive growth across the organization and leverage ERP investments for competitive advantage. Supply chain management, e-commerce and customer relationship management extensions are amongst those offering the most potential value. IBM can call upon its experience in the areas of e-business, business processes, organizational issues and ERP systems to help companies assess the potential benefits and costs of these extensions to determine which options are best aligned with their business direction.

Buy and Supply

This category addresses customer needs for sourcing and procurement of goods and services.

Supply Chain Management Services provide a suite of services that address the complex end-to-end requirements of the supply and demand chain environment. These services are focused on industry-specific client business issues such as globalization, customer value, extended enterprise and operational effectiveness. These services also address clients' needs from a supply and demand chain process view in the areas of:

- Forecasting and Demand Planning

- Strategic Sourcing and Procurement

- Customer Order Fulfillment and Customer Service

- Transportation and Shipment Management

- Distribution Network and Warehouse Operations

- Production Logistics

- Integrated Supply and Demand Chain Management

With Procurement Services, IBM provides the subject matter experts, methodologies, and assets required to help enterprises leverage e-business technologies in the effective and efficient procurement of goods and services from their suppliers. IBM provides consulting, implementation and integration offerings to help improve IBM's customer's procurement processes from sourcing through contract management to purchasing, reconciliation, and payment.

e-business Integration

This category addresses customer needs to integrate business processes and technology platforms to ensure successful implementation of multiple applications or end-to-end solutions.

Security and Privacy Services focus on security, which is the single largest concern for many businesses as they implement their e-business strategies. Here, IBM offers IT security consulting, implementation and operation services which enable customers to conduct business securely. Services cover: Security Assessment and Planning, including a workshop, security health checks, and ethical hacking testing. Security Architecture and Design, for an information asset profile, security policy definitions, standards, controls and enterprise security architecture principles, as well as guidance in designing security processes and secure Internet applications. Security Implementation, which includes detailed product analyses, selection and implementation. Security Management to provide preventative, proactive intrusion detection and emergency response to the infiltration of a private network.

Custom Systems Integration Services provide end-to-end integrated business solutions across all computing environments including host, distributed and networked computing. Here IBM offers custom-designed solutions tailored to specific business needs. IBM's systems integration services span the life cycle of a solution, from requirements analysis through solution development, installation, rollout, and end-user training. Systems integration solutions include:

- Custom application development

- Hardware and software component integration

- Application maintenance/customization/enhancement solution deployment and project management.

With Knowledge and Content Management Services, IBM helps a business understand, analyze, measure and manage a business' organization's intellectual assets, turning corporate 'wisdom' into market value. Of the 'next-generation' management disciplines now emerging, knowledge management is an essential survival requirement.

Integrated Technology Services

The emerging e-business infrastructure is a complex mosaic of high-speed networks, network-based storage systems, application servers, edge servers, wireless protocols, and standards-based platform, integration, and communication software. All of these components must work together to provide seamless computing services. As the boundaries of information technology spread beyond the individual enterprise to encompass extended, virtual enterprises, companies require an IT infrastructure that can electronically link businesses and business processes, manage growing volumes of network transactions, and connect with both wired and wireless devices.

In this broad area of service offerings, IBM offers businesses help installing, maintaining and optimizing their IT infrastructures and in managing the complexity of multivendor technology environments. IBM's Integrated Technology Services works to ensure the reliability of systems and networks, maximize the efficiency and flexibility of the IT infrastructure. Services in this segment also help secure networks and Internet transactions, provide support and training to IT departments and end users, and maintains computer and server hardware, software and networks.

These services improve the value of businesses' core technology systems and enable them to pursue new e-business initiatives. Let's look at some example services for this segment.

IT Consulting

IBM's IT Consulting Services help businesses get the most from their information technology resources, helping ensure that the technology resources not only support a business' overall objectives, but also become a strategic asset.

Total Systems Management

Total Systems Management fills the gap between traditional hardware/software maintenance and strategic IT outsourcing by providing a complete systemswide solution to the operational management of a company's IT activities. Through Total Systems Management, IBM offers businesses a long term technology partnership that delivers a systems-wide solution to manage the effectiveness of their increasingly complex IT infrastructure to guaranteed levels of quality and performance in support of their business objectives.

Infrastructure and Systems Management Services

Infrastructure and Systems Management Services takes an enterprise-wide, consultative approach to help a business manage their host-centric, distributed, desktop, and network environments. IBM's services encompass the entire life cycle, from assessment, strategy and design to implementation and operational services. IBM offers expertise, methodologies and tools to help businesses manage their IT investments, improve their operations and performance, and deliver business results.

Networking and Connectivity Services

In this set of services, IBM can assist businesses in planning, implementing and supporting networking solutions, whether involving IBM or other vendor's technologies and products, including Cisco, Nortel, 3Com, etc. IBM provides assessment and strategy consulting; complex network architecture and high-level design; logical and physical design; implementation and network deployments; and on-going network management services. Through IBM's alliance with Cisco, they can provide integrated solutions that address a business' e-business requirements and deliver the needed e-business networking infrastructure.

Business Continuity and Recovery Services

These services allow IBM to apply the business and technological expertise necessary to help keep a business running. They help businesses sift through the layers of complexity in their business and IT infrastructures to provide a fail safe continuity plan, and implementation to whatever degree of completeness companies desire, in order to keep a business fueled with the information they deem critical. Services include business continuity and recovery consulting, business risk management and advisory services, multivendor recovery,

IT recovery, critical business process continuity, and total continuity program management.

Technical Support Services

Technical Support Services includes hardware and software support services; hardware and software planning, design, installation, relocation, and migration services, site services for IT facilities, and power protection services to address electrical and mechanical environment protection needs. IBM provides hardware support for IBM and other leading manufacturers' systems and peripherals, including preventive and predictive maintenance, on-site and depot repair, and electronic systems support options. IBM also offers software support for IBM system software and middleware as well as selected services for multivendor software.

IT Consolidation Services

IT Consolidation Services helps businesses plan, implement and manage consolidations of their servers, data, and applications; networks and Storage Area Networks (SANs); physical locations; and IT support organizations and management systems. These consolidations may be triggered by a merger or acquisition, internal re-organizations, or deployment of new business applications, significant and challenging events for a business. IBM's services help ensure a smooth transition without impact to current business operations and help businesses achieve their planned IT cost reductions and performance improvements.

MidRange Express

Midrange Express for AS/400 (MRX/400) is a set of cost-effective, packaged services designed to help small and medium businesses run their AS/400(s). MRX/400 allows companies to supplement their in-house IT with IBM services, eliminating the need to hire and train additional support staff or divert internal IT resources from core business projects. With this service, businesses gain fast access to IBM's existing AS/400 operational infrastructure—the skills, facilities, and resources necessary to operate, house, and support an AS/400.

Strategic Outsourcing Services

Dramatic shifts in IT and the business landscape have transformed outsourcing from a cost-effective means of data center management to an integral part of a company's business strategy. Strategic outsourcing enables companies to offload more and more of their technology systems and processes so that they can focus on core competencies and business priorities.

IBM's Strategic Outsourcing Services works closely with businesses to evaluate their objectives and identify the processes and IT operations they can outsource for competitive advantage. Strategic outsourcing frees a business from the worries of keeping up with rapid technology changes, continually retraining their work force and retaining talent in a marketplace where IT skills are in short supply.

As companies migrate business processes to the Internet, they can use IBM's Web hosting capabilities to support Web-based applications and transactions, as well as storage requirements. A business can choose from a broad spectrum of hosting options, ranging from simple colocation to complex, integrated Web-hosting solutions, to application service provider platforms. IBM is the world's largest and most-experienced hosting services provider, with 73,000 servers under management at 133 data centers worldwide. Fifteen centers focus exclusively on e-business hosting. In partnership with AT&T, KPNQwest, and Qwest, IBM is opening 65 additional e-business hosting centers across the U.S. and Europe.

Learning Services

Learning Services supports IBM Global Services' three principal lines of business by helping businesses design, develop and deploy education and training curricula. Learning Services helps people transform their businesses by helping employees develop the skills to compete effectively in a technology-driven economy.

Capitalizing on the latest distributed learning technologies, IBM delivers Web-based solutions that enable businesses to broaden the scope of education and training, and to reduce the travel and productivity costs associated with traditional classroom training. IBM has migrated almost a third of its internal education and training to the Web, at a savings of some $50 million this year. IBM estimates that it can avoid $400,000 in education costs for every 1000 classroom days converted to distributed learning.

Index

Reader Feedback Sheet

Your comments and suggestions are very important in shaping future publications. Please email us at *moreinfo@maxpress.com* or photocopy this page, jot down your thoughts, and fax it to (850) 934-9981 or mail it to:

Maximum Press

Attn: Jim Hoskins

605 Silverthorn Road

Gulf Breeze, FL 32561

_____

_____

_____

_____

_____

_____

_____

_____

_____

_____

_____

_____

_____

_____

_____

_____

_____

_____

_____

_____

*101 Ways to Promote
Your Web Site
Second Edition*
by Susan Sweeney, C.A.
552 pages
$29.95
ISBN: 1-885068-45-X

*Marketing
With E-Mail
Second Edition*
by Shannon Kinnard
352 pages
$29.95
ISBN: 1-885068-51-4

*Business-to-Business
Internet Marketing,
Third Edition*
by Barry Silverstein
528 pages
$29.95
ISBN: 1-885068-50-6

*Marketing on
the Internet,
Fifth Edition*
by Jan Zimmerman
512 pages
$34.95
ISBN: 1-885068-49-2

*Internet Marketing
for Information
Technology
Companies*
by Barry Silverstein
464 pages
$39.95
ISBN: 1-885068-46-8

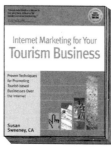

*Internet Marketing
for Your Tourism
Business*
by Susan Sweeney, C.A.
592 pages
$39.95
ISBN: 1-885068-47-6

*Building Intranets
with Lotus Notes &
Domino, 5.0,
Third Edition*
by Steve Krantz
320 pages
$39.95
ISBN: 1-885068-41-7

*Internet Marketing for
Less Than $500/Year*
by Marcia Yudkin
334 pages
$29.95
ISBN: 1-885068-52-2

To purchase a Maximum Press book, visit your local bookstore
or call 1-800-989-6733 (US) or 1-850-934-4583 (International)
online ordering available at *www.maxpress.com*

*Exploring IBM
RS/6000 Computers,
Tenth Edition*
by Jim Hoskins
and Doug Davies
440 pages
$39.95
ISBN: 1-885068-42-5

*Exploring IBM @server
iSeries and AS/400
Computers,
Tenth Edition*
by Jim Hoskins and
Roger Dimmick
560 pages
$39.95
ISBN: 1-885068-43-3

*Exploring IBM
S/390 Computers,
Sixth Edition*
by Jim Hoskins
and George Coleman
472 pages
$39.95
ISBN: 1-885068-30-1

*Exploring IBM
Network Stations*
by Eddie Ho,
Dana Lloyd, and
Stephanos Heracleous
223 pages
$39.95
ISBN: 1-885068-32-8

*Exploring IBM
@server xSeries
and PCs,
Eleventh Edition*
by Jim Hoskins
and Bill Wilson
384 pages
$39.95
ISBN: 1-885068-39-5

*Exploring IBM
Technology, Products
& Services,
Fourth Edition*
edited by Jim Hoskins
256 pages
$54.95
ISBN: 1-885068-44-1

To purchase a Maximum Press book, visit your local bookstore
or call 1-800-989-6733 (US/Canada) or 1-850-934-4583 (International)
online ordering available at *www.maxpress.com*